To mom at Christmas 1977
from Wilbur & Dolores

May Love, Peace, and Joy be yours
through every season of the new year.

The Family Album

★ ★
★ ★ ★
★ ★ ★ ★
★ ★ ★
★ ★

The Family Album

Edited by
ARTHUR AND NANCY DeMOSS

Associate Editor
JOSEPH V. GORMAN

Illustrations by
JOSEPH L. VOELKER

Published by
A. J. HOLMAN COMPANY
Division of J. B. Lippincott Company
Philadelphia and New York

ACKNOWLEDGMENTS

Grateful acknowledgment is hereby expressed to all those who have contributed to this book. Any inadvertent omissions of credit will be gladly corrected in future editions.

ABINGDON PRESS for "Happy Thanksgiving" from *Thanksgiving, Feast and Festival* by Mildred Corell Luckhardt. Copyright © 1966 by Abingdon Press. Also, for "Month for Waking" from *Petals Of Light* by Jane Merchant. Poem copyright © 1963 assigned to Abingdon Press. Used by permission.

AMERICAN BAPTIST BOARD OF EDUCATION AND PUBLICATION for "A Thirsty Soul" by Twyla Wood from *The Secret Place*. Used by permission of the American Baptist Board of Education and Publication.

CURTIS BROWN, LTD. for "Firelight" from *Sundial Of The Seasons* by Hal Borland. Reprinted by permission of Curtis Brown, Ltd. Copyright © 1964 by Hal Borland.

CHRISTIAN HERALD for "Brighten Up the Downhill Side of Winter" by John J. Breen. Copyright © 1972 by Christian Herald.

CHRISTIAN HERITAGE for "I Knew Columbus" by Evelyn Witter.

DAVID C. COOK PUBLISHING CO. for "Fire" and "The Poor Little Rich King". Reprinted from *The Poor Little Rich King*, Copyright © 1973, David C. Cook Publishing Co., Elgin, IL 60120. Used by permission.

RUPERT CREW LIMITED for "Golden Verse" by Patience Strong.

DECISION for "Golden Thought" by Franz Joseph Haydn from *Decision*. Also, "His Eye Is On The Sparrow"—Poetry by Terry Germain Free, May 1976 from *Decision*, Copyright © 1976 by the Billy Graham Evangelistic Association. Also, "Heaven Revisited" from *Decision*, Copyright © 1971 by the Billy Graham Evangelistic Association.

ACKNOWLEDGMENTS continued on page 176

Contents

Editors' Foreword

This year as we began making selections for *The Family Album,* we became aware of the fact that there are always new and beautiful ways to praise Jesus Christ. The supply of verses and stories seems inexhaustible, just as Jesus' love is inexhaustible.

Not every piece in this volume mentions Jesus by name. Yet the poets and writers whose works we have chosen still praise Him by making such creative use of the talents He gave them.

What a gift to be able to affect other people deeply by the written word! Nancy and I think that this year's selections are especially inspirational. They have provided us with many moments of comfort and meditation, and we hope you will also enjoy reflecting on them.

As always, let me wholeheartedly extend the invitation to write to us with your comments. We are grateful for your interest, and we delight in hearing from you.

Sincerely,
Arthur and Nancy DeMoss

The Family Album

BOOKS, LIKE PROVERBS, RECEIVE THEIR CHIEF VALUE
FROM THE STAMP AND ESTEEM OF AGES THROUGH
WHICH THEY PASSED.

temple

The New Year

this month shall be unto you the beginning of
months: it shall be the first month
of the year to you.

EXODUS 12:2

Firelight

Say what you will about January—which hasn't a mere two faces, like its mythological namesake, but a full thirty-one—it makes a man happy to be the owner of a roof and a fire. And to have someone to share them. January is for companionship. January justifies the overworked word "cozy," which itself comes from the cold Norse countries where kose sig meant to make one's self comfortable.

Mid-January seems to have been put in the year to provide fireside evenings, leisurely reading, quiet, friendly talk. The simpler inner resources, so easily glossed over when the world is full of golden sunlight, green shade and soft Summer starlight, now come into their own. One feels no urgency to be gregarious or full of busy, bright, warm-weather chatter. One needs only to toss a log on the fire, find an easy chair, and let the heart do its own talking, in its own time.

It's a strange paradox that the warmth of friendship so often runs an inverse ratio to the height of the mercury in the thermometer. Cold nights call for close friends, and the number is important primarily as a limitation. No lawn party groups now, no houseful, but rather the intimate few. And the talk now has range and depth rather than deftness and volume. Thoughts seem to prosper in a warm room with a cold wind at the door.

Snow and ice clarify the mind as well as the air, and firelight better illuminates the reason than moonlight. Maybe that's one reason for living in a latitude where Winter has a degree of authority; it gives a man time to explore his thoughts, to look at his own heart and to approach understanding.

Hal Borland

Winter Takes A Bow!

Winter is the grand finale
Scheduled to appear
Just before the closing curtain
Of another year.
And beneath the icy spotlights,
Standing center-stage,
Once again she proves performance
Grows refined with age.

Prima Donna of the seasons,
Winter holds her own,
Crystal slippers gleaming brightly
'Neath a snowflake gown.
Radiant beneath the shelter
Of her frosty hood,
Blending with the silver shadows
Of a quiet wood.

Winter is the leading lady
In a grand review,
Smiling at the acclamation
She's accustomed to.
Poised before the scenic backdrop
Ermine hills allow,
Never did a finer actress
. . . Take a greater bow!

Grace E. Easley

His Wondrous Ways

O God,
I thank you for the seasons
and the change they bring
from the cold and snow of Winter
to life-renewing Spring,
through the growing months of Summer
to the showy Autumn days
that speak of purpose in your planning
and your loving
wondrous ways. AMEN.

Paul Hamsher

Take Time

Take time to think —
    It is the source of power.
Take time to give —
    It is too short a day to be selfish.
Take time to play —
    It is the secret of perpetual youth.
Take time to read —
    It is the fountain of wisdom.
Take time to pray —
    It is the greatest power on earth.
Take time to love and be loved —
    It is a God given privilege.
Take time to laugh —
    It is the music of the soul.
Take time to work —
    It is the price of success.
Take time to be friendly —
    It is the road to happiness.

Author Unknown

Second Chance

The Christmas holidays are over. You've put away the gifts; you've tried the new color TV; you've totaled the cost of keeping up with the crowd; and you're suddenly stung with a sense of guilt. You were having such a good time celebrating Christmas that you gave very little time to the Christ of Christmas.

How wonderful that God gives Christmas another chance when we fail him! However much we've failed in the past, the coming of the New Year is an ideal time to start all over again.

Life is full of beginnings, and today is the first day of the rest of your life. Go back to where you left Him—He's waiting for you.

Eunice Fields

Winter Dawn

Across the morning sky we see,
In flaming colors drawn,
A masterpiece of nature's art,—
A frosty morn at dawn.

Lavender and yellow blend
With purple, orange and red;
Flamboyant colors, tier on tier,
Across the heavens spread.

The sun ascends beyond the rim,
To stand in dazzling view,
While colors slowly fade into
A sea of morning dew.

Joy fills the heart and feeds the soul,
When, on a winter morn,
Emblazoned by His handiwork,
Another day is born.

Esther Lee Carter

Be Still — And Know

Sometimes we have an experience so moving, so soul-stirring, that we want to share it with the world.

Such an experience was mine one day last winter when there was an ice storm, complete with furious lashing wind and angry freezing torrents of rain. Trees and weeds slanted in a westerly direction, bent by the wind and immobilized within a coat of ice. After the storm subsided, I walked out our lane, or more accurately—I slip-slid carefully—for the lane also wore an overcoat of ice.

I stopped to observe the ice-sheathed scene, a tarnished-silver, gray world under a leaden-gray sky. Gusts of wind shook the trees, sending showers of icy slivers to the ground, where they bounced with a hollow, pattering sound. As I watched and listened, I became conscious of a trickle of water. From 'way back in the field there was a crackly sound, and with it a tinkling and trickling of many small rivulets of water. The wave of sound moved toward me, passed, and faded away.

Trickling waves of sound continued to approach and subside, yet there was no change in the appearance of the field. All motion was beneath the blanket of ice. More gusts of wind playfully shook more ice slivers from the trees, the ice skittering and dancing over the ice-frosted woods' floor. After the roaring wind and pounding rain, these were playful sounds, springtime-in-the-middle-of-winter sounds. I wished everyone in the world could hear the happy tinkling.

And then I realized the impossibility of such a wish. For if a crowd could be gathered to hear such delicate, fragile sounds, those sounds would be lost in the shuffle of feet, the clearing of throats, the murmur and rustle of clothing, no matter how subdued.

Maybe the small, quiet sounds of nature are meant to be experienced in solitude. Not only because it's the only way we can hear their fragile tones, but because in solitude we have time to think about the things of nature—and of the nature of man.

The noise of a storm crowds out the stillness needed for contemplation. The activity of a storm causes us to rush about closing windows, checking garage doors, too busy to think of anything except the task at hand. The threat of a storm makes us single-minded.

Only in quiet aloneness can we fully comprehend the command to "Be still and know that I am God." Psalm 46:10.

Ruby Maschke

GOldEN NUGGET

Time

Time cannot be possessed
you know, it slips
between our fingertips
like grains of sand
upon a beach. . . .
Use it before it slips!

Miriam Woolfolk

Snow At Dusk

Feather-soft snow
Descends with evening's dusk,
And with gentle hands
Tucks the earth to bed
Beneath a blanket
Of silvery silence.

Mark Bullock

A New Year's Wish

May you always have:
Enough happiness to keep you pleasant . . .
Enough trials to challenge you . . .
Enough sorrow to make you compassionate.
Enough success to urge you on . . .
Enough failure to maintain your humility . . .
Enough health to keep you smiling . . .
Enough friends to share life with . . .
Enough wealth to meet your needs . . .
Enough faith to sustain you . . .
Enough work for your hands and mind . . .
Enough love to fill every corner of your heart.

Author Unknown

GOLDEN THOUGHT

Lost time is never found again.

Benjamin Franklin

Winter Warfare

In clear shining armor the fir trees stand
  Ready to battle the snows.
Wearing fine breastplates and icicle swords
  They march toward the storm in rows.

Brave soldiers are they like warriors of old
  Girded in combat array—
Invincible legions until with the dawn
  The sun melts their armor away.

Jean Conder Soule

This New Year, God

Give us, O God, the grace we need . . . To live this new year right . . . With faith and hope and trust in You . . . Each morning, noon and night . . . Inspire us to nobler heights . . . Of love and charity . . . Unto our smallest neighbor and . . . Our tallest enemy . . . Endow us with the wisdom and . . . The courage that we need . . . To serve You loyally, O God . . . In thought and word and deed . . . Without your help there is no help . . . That we can ever give . . . Without Your gift of air to breathe . . . We could not even live . . . And when temptation trips us and . . . We stumble on our way . . . Forgive us, God, and help us up . . . To start a better day.

James J. Metcalfe

Brighten Up The Downhill Side Of Winter

At the onset of one heavy snow storm last year, my wife phoned a friend who lives in an old farm house two miles from a paved road to ask if she and her family would care to spend the night at our house.

"It's such a terrible night," my wife began.

"But it's a wonderful night," came the friend's excited reply. "Just think. By morning we'll be snowed in!"

Her family, she explained, looked forward each year at this time to being snowbound on their gravel country road. Such a day was unexpected and treasured—A "Found Day," her family had come to call it.

"The first time we realized we were snowed in," she said, "we were well into our weekday morning routine. Bob was preparing his shower, Nancy just had to quickly iron her pleated skirt, Scott was searching the den for the homework he had 'put right there', and I was making coffee, offering encouragement to Nancy and wondering how I would fit in the marketing between the hairdresser and the dentist. Then Scott shouted, 'Hey, lookit the snow out there!'

"Each of us stopped what we were doing, went to the window and for one silent moment watched the wind drive the still-falling snow. When we turned from the window, something very strange and very wonderful started to happen to us.

"Bob got dressed and with Scott went to the shed for firewood. Nancy unplugged the iron, folded her half-pressed skirt and began checking our supply of candles and filling buckets with water in case of a power failure. I forgot my crowded schedule, and, after checking our supply of canned goods, changed our breakfasts from the usual toast, juice and a dash for the door to grapefruit, pancakes and sausages.

"That one look out the window—the realization that no one was going to be able to do what he wanted to do had completely changed 'Is my breakfast ready?' and 'Where are my socks?' to 'Let me help you with that' and 'Can I get anything else for you, Mom?' "

It is much more satisfying to ask, "May I help you?" than to complain, "Isn't mine ready yet, Mom?" Since that first snow, her family considers January and February a disappointment if they're not snowed in at least once to celebrate the "anniversary" of their discovery.

What our neighbor was excited about, of course, was her family's discovery that each member can get so wrapped up in thinking about what he or she needs that family life as a unit often gets neglected. A sudden storm on the downhill side of winter made them rediscover together the "something wonderful" that they are careful now to nurture all year long.

John J. Breen

We Lift Up Our Eyes
Unto The Hills - - -

and the stars and the moon make each snow crystal glisten and gleam - - - the graceful branches of the elms and birch are lined with white - - - the little bird's nest is overflowing - - - Blankets of snow cover the spruce - - - leaving only an edging of green - - -

- - - the wind is still - - -

and in the stillness is music - - - deep - - - wondrous harmony - - - playing to the heart that is attune - - - listening - - - and dreaming - - -

Whether this is imagination or not - - one never really knows - - - and it matters little - - - for in that moment - - - ecstasy holds the soul - - -

Gwen Frostic

A New Year's Garden

For this year's winning garden
Plant four straight rows of peas.
Politeness, and Preparedness,
The very first of these.
Next, Patience in a tender row,
(Please cultivate with care.)
Then on your knees, most earnestly,
Plant one long row of Prayer.
Five fertile rows of lettuce sow;
Let us be kind and true.
Let us be faithful to the tasks
That we are called to do.
Let us forgive our fellowmen;
Let us our blessings share.
Let us be thankful. What a crop
One little plot will bear.

Pearl Polosky

Easter

lo, the winter is past...the time
of the singing of birds is come.

song of solomon 2:11,12

The Book

I opened the Book and it spoke
　　to me.
It said, "Come for an hour to
　　Galilee."
I met twelve men who held in
　　their hands
Man's destiny ever in far flung
　　lands.

I watched with the Master on
　　Olive's brow;
And came back a wiser one some-
　　how.
I wept at the cross on Calvary's
　　hill;
Saw Mary mourn for her Son so
　　still.

I closed the pages of my good
　　friend
And found, that at my journey's
　　end,
My life could ne'er again be
　　the same;
Once I had linked it with His
　　name.

Lucille Crumley

Spring

Open the windows,
Swing wide the doors
And hear the birds' cadences ring;
Let golden sunlight
And soft breezes tune
Your heart to the great song of spring!

Ice-covered waters
Aroused by spring's kiss,
In silvery laughter run free;
Their joy awakens
The flowers from dreams,
Divine in their gay artistry.

The seal of winter
Has broken away,
And out of earth's tomb comes new life;
Spring now brings release,
And the blessings of peace
To hearts held in bondage and strife.

Dorothy M. Cahoon

For My Lord

The Dogwood, white, is bursting forth
To greet the Easter Morn.

Forsythia, golden, for the king,
Replace His crown of thorns.

Violets, purple, for His robes
To hail His coronation.

And red, the poppies in the field
To mark His Resurrection.

Marianna Rossi Decker

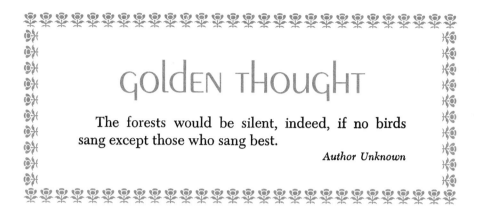

GOLDEN THOUGHT

The forests would be silent, indeed, if no birds sang except those who sang best.

Author Unknown

Month For Waking

We waken early
Lest some rose
Should bloom without
Our supervision,
Or some unpracticed
Maple leaf
Escape applause
For its precision
In following
Prescribed design
In every dainty
Jiggled line.

We stay up late
Lest a moon light
In an apple tree
With petaled glowing,
Or mockingbird
Pour liquid stars
From flooded throat
Without our knowing.
Sleep is a waste,
Absurd, extreme,
When May is all
One waking dream.

Jane Merchant

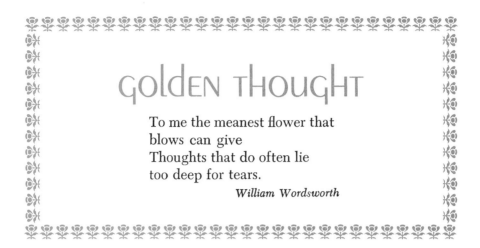

The Willow

The willow shakes her tousled locks
And runs a wind-comb through her hair;
Then preening by the glass-like pond
She chooses April's green to wear.

Jean Conder Soule

The Watchmen Saw It Happen

Jesus was dead. There was no doubt about it. His enemies had seized him in the night while he was praying in a garden and had nailed him on a cross. There he had died. His friends had buried him in a new tomb of rock and had rolled a mighty rock before the entrance.

His enemies knew that Jesus had promised his disciples that he would rise again from the dead and that they would see him and know him. So, to be sure that the disciples did not come and steal away the body of Jesus and claim that he was alive still, they had gone to Pilate, the Roman governor.

"Your excellency," they had demanded when they stood before Pilate, "when this Jesus was still alive he promised his disciples that he would arise again from the dead in three days. Command that a guard of Roman soldiers be placed on guard before the tomb, lest the disciples of Jesus try to steal his body and then tell the people that he has risen from the dead. We want the people to forget that this man ever lived. How in the world can we accomplish such a thing if the story goes around that he is still alive?"

"Very well," Pilate agreed. "Take a guard of soldiers and make the tomb of Jesus as secure as you can. Here is the great Roman seal with which to seal the rock before the doorway. No one would dare break that!"

So off went the elders and placed the soldier guard on watch. To make things doubly sure, they fixed the heavy rock with the great Roman seal that no man dared break for fear of his life. Then, satisfied at last, the enemies of Jesus went home. Now they were sure that no one would dare to tamper with the tomb and that the people would soon forget all about Jesus. Had they not declared that Jesus was a fraud and an impostor? Had they not said that he was a criminal and had they not put him to death? Who would want to follow the teachings of a dead criminal?

But the enemies of Jesus were not prepared for what happened. There was a day of grief. Then at dawn there was an earthquake. An angel was seen to roll away the mighty stone from before the place where Jesus lay. The broken seal fell to the ground in pieces. The stone lay beside the door. On it sat the angel who had rolled it away. He sat on the stone as though it were a garden bench!

The soldiers, when they saw the strength and beauty of God's messenger, shook and trembled. Some of them fainted with fright and fell down like dead men. Never had a Roman soldier seen anything like this. They had not seen Jesus return to life and leave the garden, but they had seen quite enough. As soon as they recovered from their fright they ran to the city and told the enemies of Jesus all that had happened.

"The earth shook under our feet," they gasped. "We saw the messenger of God come and break the great seal. He rolled away the mighty stone that blocks the door of the tomb—rolled it away as though it were a mere pebble!"

"We did!" agreed another, as breathless as the first soldier. "We saw the angel in all his strength and beauty. He sat upon the stone as one strolling through a garden comes to rest on a bench and gazes about him fearlessly."

"We were afraid," added a third soldier. "Indeed, all of us who could move, fled; the others lay like dead men in a faint."

"I shall never forget how strong the angel was," whispered a young guard, "nor how beautiful. His face shone as lightning lights up a night sky. His garments were as white as new-fallen snow. Never have we seen such a sight!"

On hearing the soldiers' report the elders and other enemies of Jesus were puzzled and troubled. "Surely these men are mad," some cried and angrily forbade them to say anything more about it.

Continued on page 24

Continued from page 23

"But they are excited and cannot keep still," protested one of the elders. "Suppose their story gets out to the people!"

"We must do something about this," decided another in the group. "Let us pay these men a great sum of money to keep them from spreading this ridiculous story." Then, turning to the soldiers, he ordered them not to repeat what they had told the group. "Instead, tell all whom you meet that the disciples of this man Jesus came in the night and stole his body while you slept. We will make it worth your while to do this," and he named a great sum of money that they would give to them if they would repeat this lie.

"But the stone was too great for so few men to roll it away," the captain of the guard protested. "Anyone who sees the stone will see that and say that such a thing is impossible."

"What about the broken seal?" breathed one soldier, trembling. "Everyone knows only an angel would dare to break that!"

"Besides, we saw it happen," the youngest guard reminded the group. "Our report is true."

"And what will the governor do if we say that we slept while we were on guard? It is death for a soldier to sleep at his post."

"Don't worry about that," said the elders. "If this comes to the governor's ears, we will speak to him for you. We will see that you have no trouble about the matter."

So, though they were much afraid, the soldiers greedily accepted the money offered to them, for the portion that came to each guard was a great sum. They went out and followed the instructions that had been given to them. To everyone who asked, they answered as with one voice, "His disciples came at night while we slept and stole away the body of their Master." And this was the story the enemies of Jesus told to everyone.

But the disciples of Jesus knew better. They had seen the risen Christ! They had talked to him and had heard him speak to them. "Jesus lives!" they cried joyfully on meeting one another. "He is alive forevermore."

That is why Easter is the happiest day of all to the friends of Jesus. They know he is near wherever they go and that he hears them when they speak to him. Jesus promised that because he lives, we who love him shall live also. He overcame death and evil for us that we might be where he is. This is his promise, and God whose Spirit was in Jesus always keeps his promises. That is why we make our churches beautiful and sing our gladdest hymns on Easter day. That is why the true friends of Jesus are brave and strong; they know there is nothing to be afraid of, no, not even death itself.

Elizabeth S. Whitehouse

The Unforgettables

It is not easy to forget
    the subtle, earthy odor
    of freshly-ploughed fields
    and orchards of peach trees,
    full-bloom.

It is not easy to forget
    the brilliance of a full moon
    at mid-night on the desert.

It is not easy to forget
    the rhythm of the sea
    that breaks against
    the biscuit-colored sand
    in shimmering, lace-edged waves,
    washed in gold.

It is not easy to forget
    a sunset, cerise
    and dusky violet
    setting a-top
    a purple mountain range.

And it is not easy to forget
    a fleecy cloudlet
    drifting overhead
    and spilling April showers . . .
    turning fields to rainbow hue!

Velta Myrle Allen

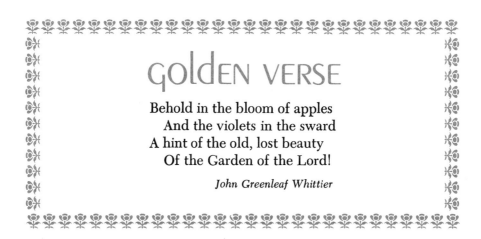

GOLDEN VERSE

Behold in the bloom of apples
    And the violets in the sward
A hint of the old, lost beauty
    Of the Garden of the Lord!

John Greenleaf Whittier

Easter

Unlike the weeks of Lent, when we abstain
from little pleasures, frost withholds, en masse
the garden flowers and the greening grass
till freed through springtime's sun and fruitful rain.

May this year's resurrection of the earth,
this Easter Day's hosannas bring to pass
hearts open to the Son; our soul's rebirth.

Katherine Paxson

A Bit Of Eternity

I saw a butterfly today
So bright, so beautiful, so gay;
Oh, how I wanted him to stay,
But he kissed a rose and flew away.

I knew a moment's bliss today;
Oh, how I wanted it to stay,
But time will harbor no delay,
So it touched my heart and slipped away.

Just the touch of a butterfly's kiss—
Just one glimpse of ecstatic bliss—
But for the rose and heart of me,
Both meant a bit of Eternity.

Helen Lowrie Marshall

Fickle April

Today blue April mourns;
At first she wailed
    as violent gusts of giant flakes
    whirled madly in the wake
      of icy winds . . .
But now, emotion spent,
She softly weeps,
    quite blinded
    as her tears drop silent
    into overflowing pools.

A pair of crows flap idly by
    in black-winged mourning;
They but add notes
    to an already drear lament:
"Today King Winter's dead!
 O weep for him!"

Tomorrow . . . grief forgot,
Her somber garb replaced
    with virgin white,
Bright April with her
    sparkling smile
    and laughter sweet
    will pay allegiance
    to the new-crowned Queen . . .
As in her path, on dancing feet,
    she gaily scatters
    springtime flowers.

Ruby Jones

GOLDEN THOUGHT

"A weed is no more than a flower in disguise."

James Russell Lowell

My God, My God, Why Hast Thou Forsaken Me?

And so Pilate, willing to content the people, released Barabbas unto them, and delivered Jesus, when he had scourged him, to be crucified.

And when they had mocked him, they took off the purple from him, and put his own clothes on him, and led him out to crucify him.

And they compel one Simon a Cyrenian, who passed by, coming out of the country, the father of Alexander and Rufus, to bear his cross.

And they bring him unto the place Golgotha, which is, being interpreted, The place of a skull.

And they gave him to drink wine mingled with myrrh: but he received it not.

And when they had crucified him, they parted his garments, casting lots upon them, what every man should take.

And it was the third hour, and they crucified him.

And the superscription of his accusation was written over, THE KING OF THE JEWS.

And with him they crucify two thieves; the one on his right hand, and the other on his left.

And when the sixth hour was come, there was darkness over the whole land until the ninth hour.

And at the ninth hour Jesus cried with a loud voice, saying, Eloi, Eloi, lamasabachthani? which is, being interpreted, My God, my God, why hast thou forsaken me?

And some of them that stood by, when they heard it, said, Behold, he calleth Elias.

And one ran and filled a sponge full of vinegar, and put it on a reed, and gave him to drink, saying, Let alone; let us see whether Elias will come to take him down.

And Jesus cried with a loud voice, and gave up the ghost.

And the veil of the temple was rent in twain from the top to the bottom.

And when the centurion, which stood over against him, saw that he so cried out, and gave up the ghost, he said, Truly this man was the Son of God.

St. Mark 15

He Is Risen...

And when the sabbath was past, Mary Magdalene, and Mary the mother of James, and Salome, had bought sweet spices, that they might come and anoint him.

And very early in the morning the first day of the week, they came unto the sepulchre at the rising of the sun.

And they said among themselves, Who shall roll us away the stone from the door of the sepulchre?

And when they looked, they saw that the stone was rolled away: for it was very great.

And entering into the sepulchre, they saw a young man sitting on the right side, clothed in a long white garment; and they were affrighted.

And he saith unto them, Be not affrighted: Ye seek Jesus of Nazareth, which was crucified: he is risen; he is not here: behold the place where they laid him.

But go your way, tell his disciples and Peter that he goeth before you into Galilee: there shall ye see him, as he said unto you.

And they went out quickly, and fled from the sepulchre; for they trembled and were amazed: neither said they any thing to any man; for they were afraid.

Afterward he appeared unto the eleven as they sat at meat, and upbraided them with their unbelief and hardness of heart, because they believed not them which had seen him after he was risen.

St. Mark 16

Then the eleven disciples went away into Galilee, into a mountain where Jesus had appointed them.

And when they saw him, they worshipped him: but some doubted.

And Jesus came and spake unto them, saying, All power is given unto me in heaven and in earth.

Go ye therefore, and teach all nations, baptizing them in the name of the Father, and of the Son, and of the Holy Ghost:

Teaching them to observe all things whatsoever I have commanded you: and, lo, I am with you always, even unto the end of the world. Amen.

St. Matthew 28

Nostalgia

Oh it is strange how southern mountains call
With the first sign of spring! Flame azaleas
Will soon be in bloom and a waterfall
Will sparkle and wild honeybees will buzz,
As they make mountain laurel honey for
Little bears and boys to find. Then will come
Dogwood, roses and wild orchids galore
And great clusters of bright rhododendron.
The calico bush in its summer dress
Will vie with pink flowering tobacco
On every small mountain farm, and I guess
As long as I live I shall have to go
Where I can hear the sad nightingale's song
And roam the mountain trails the summer long!

Louise Justice

Footprints In The Snow

Spring tiptoed thru the town last night,
Disguised in robes of winter-white.
This morning she seems far away—
The wind so cold—the skies so grey—
But there are signs that prove it so,
Small crocus footprints in the snow!

Helen Lowrie Marshall

April Rain

The wild sweet rain of April spills
On golden-throated daffodils,
On garden wall and new green bough,
On earth fresh-turned before the plough.

It scrubs the pansy's small shy face
And shines each blade of grass in place
To leave the springtime world aglow,
And lift my heart to walk tiptoe.

Viney Wilder

Rare Beauty

Roses grow where planted
Giving freely
Of rare beauty
To all who pass.
When the beautys' gone
The fragrance lingers long
Upon the path.

Loretta Bowser

Lilacs

O delicate sweetness in lavender
    gowns,
While modestly wearing your young
    April crowns,
You garnish my garden with spring's
    gentle graces,
And O how you brighten my friends'
    winter faces!

Virginia Vess

The Gladness Of May

Then, sing ye birds, sing, sing a
    joyous song!
    And let the young lambs bound
    As to the tabor's sound!
We, in thought, will join your
    throng,
    Ye that pipe and ye that play,
    Ye that through your hearts
    to-day
Feel the gladness of the May!

William Wordsworth

Mrs. McMinney And Her Children

Up the hill, a hop and two skips from Blue Water Brook, lived Mrs. McMinney and her four problem children. They weren't bad children. It was just that they preferred to play instead of work.

"Please feed the chickens some corn," Mrs. McMinney would say to her little son, Teddy.

Teddy would head for the chicken coop, but on the way he'd stop to dig a few holes in his sandpile. And that is where he'd spend the rest of the day, forgetting all about the hungry chickens.

"Please get a bucket of water for tea," Mrs. McMinney would say to her younger daughter, Frannie.

Frannie would run happily to Blue Water Brook. But she'd soon be wading and splashing while the empty bucket sat on the bank.

"Please get some wood for the fire," Mrs. McMinney would say to her older son, Hank.

Hank would get as far as the apple tree. There he'd eat one apple after another until he'd have a stomachache and be too sick to carry a heavy load of wood.

"Please run to the village and buy some flour to bake bread," Mrs. McMinney would say to her older daughter, Alice.

Alice would start across the meadow. But she'd just have to stop to pick a bouquet of wild flowers. Then she'd decide to make a garland of them. And so it would go until sundown. By then it was too late to go to the village.

Mrs. McMinney sat beside the cold fireplace with no water for tea or flour for bread. Outside, the hungry hens clucked angrily.

"I must find some way to teach my children to work," she said.

She thought and thought. At last, she had an idea.

Early the next morning, she carried a spade to the sandbox where Teddy was making sand tunnels.

"Teddy-lad," she said, "here is a nice big shovel to play with."

"Oh, thank you, Mother, but it is too big for my sandbox."

"Well, well," said Mrs. McMinney, "so it is. Why don't you dig in this nice patch of black soil instead?"

Teddy liked that idea. He dug and dug until he had the patch of soil loosened and soft.

Late that night, when the children were in bed, Mrs. McMinney planted rows of peas, lettuce, carrots, and radishes in the soil.

"Frannie-love," Mrs. McMinney said to her younger daughter two weeks later, "I have a new toy for you."

She handed Frannie a yellow watering can.

"It's lovely, Mother," said Frannie. "How does it work?"

"Fill it with water at the brook," instructed Mrs. McMinney. "Then pour the water through the spout onto the patch of soft black soil."

"That will be fun!" giggled Frannie in delight.

Soon the vegetables in the little garden patch began to grow. And so did the weeds.

"Alice, dear," said Mrs. McMinney, "I know where there are some lovely little green plants you could pick and weave into long ropes."

"Where? Oh, where?" Alice asked eagerly.

Mrs. McMinney pointed to the weeds in the garden.

"But don't pick the plants that are growing in rows," she warned.

All summer long, Teddy played with his spade in the garden, keeping the soil soft.

Frannie played with her watering can, so the plants had enough moisture.

Alice picked every weed to make pretty long ropes. That gave the vegetables plenty of room to grow.

"Hank, my son," said Mrs. McMinney one summer day, "how would you like some fresh peas and lettuce and carrots and radishes?"

"Mmmm! I'd love some," Hank replied.

"There are lots of them growing on those plants in that patch of nice black soil," said Mrs. McMinney. "Help yourself, and bring all you can't eat into the house."

Hank and the rest of the family enjoyed delicious fresh vegetables for supper that night. Then Mrs. McMinney sat back and smiled at her children.

"These certainly are fine vegetables you raised," she said.

"We raised them?" they asked, looking at each other in surprise.

"Yes," replied Mrs. McMinney. "You raised them in that patch of soil you spaded, watered, weeded, and harvested."

The children smiled proudly.

"Oh, it was easy," said Teddy.

"It was fun," said Frannie.

"We'll do it again next year," said Alice.

"And make it even bigger," added Hank.

And they did!

Marilyn Kratz

Daffodils In The Rain

Nothing I have ever seen
Is lovelier than silver rain
Falling on gold daffodils
In bloom along my garden lane.

Overnight they have appeared,
As if by magic, from the ground.
Grateful for their first rain bath,
They revel in its friendly sound.

William Arnette Wofford

The Rain

When you hear the splashing rain,
    Does your heart stand still,
As you think of the rivers
    That the raindrops fill,
And the leaping, snapping fishes
    That go swirling there,
And water lilies looking up
    To wash their faces fair?

And in the marshes, cowslips
    Nod their yellow heads,
And frogs go "Chug-a-rum"
    Upon their damp, green beds.
In meadows, wee blue violets
    Look up in shy surprise;
Worm-hunting robins cock their heads
    And blink their beady eyes.

So do not sit and fret
    When you hear the tapping rain;
It's bringing life and loveliness
    To river, hill, and plain;
And when the sun comes out again,
    Your eyes, with joy, will see
How God has made the world anew
    For creatures—and for Thee!

Beulah H. Ragland

Heritage Plantation, Sandwich, Cape Cod, Massachusetts

Home and Family

house and riches are the inheritance of fathers:
and a prudent wife is from the Lord.

PROVERBS 19:14

A Bit Of Paradise

I stood upon the highest hill
And saw my town below,
A little doll-house village
Replaced the one I know.
The streets were crossing ribbons
With houses lining these,
The little brook a winding line
Among the fields and trees.

The lake a shining mirror
Reflecting bits of sky
And in the canopy above
White clouds were floating by.
The apple trees all pink and white
Were each a small bouquet
And the lawns were little patches
With tiny dolls at play.

Toy animals in meadows grazed
Or rested near the wood;
My town displayed in miniature—
I saw that it was good.
The sunshine bathed it all in gold
For beauty quite supreme
And I was King of the mountain
As I realized a dream.

Continued on page 38

Continued from page 37

I'd watched the road go up the hill
Until it touched the sky
And hoped some day to follow it
When I had time to try.
While it hadn't led to Heaven
Where it had seemed to go,
All my efforts were rewarded
By the paradise below.

All the dear familiar places
I knew so very well
Had suddenly gained in value
Beneath a magic spell.
I searched and found the schoolhouse,
The church and rising steeple
And I realized I loved this town
And all the friendly people.

Harriet Whipple

Dream House

Let there be within these phantom walls
Beauty where the hearth fire's shadow falls . . .
Quiet pictures—books—and welcoming chairs . . .
Music that the very silence shares . . .
Kitchen windows curtained blue and white . . .
Shelves and cupboards built for my delight . . .
Little things that lure and beckon me
With their tranquil joy! And let there be
Lilt of laughter—swift-forgotten tears
Woven through the fabric of the years . . .
Strength to guard me—eyes to answer mine,
Mutely clear. And though without may shine
Stars of dawn or sunset's wistful glow—
All of life and love my house shall know!

Catherine Parmenter Newell

Prayer For This House

May nothing evil cross this door,
And may ill fortune never pry
About these windows; may the roar
    And rain go by.

Strengthened by faith, these rafters will
Withstand the batt'ring of the storm;
This hearth, though all the world grow chill,
    Will keep us warm.

Peace shall walk softly through these rooms,
Touching our lips with holy wine,
Till ev'ry casual corner blooms
    Into a shrine.

Laughter shall drown the raucous shout;
And, though these shelt'ring walls are thin,
May they be strong to keep hate out
    And hold love in.

Louis Untermeyer

The Road

There used to be a winding road
    That went right past my door;
And I would long to follow it
    And travel the world o'er.

Now that I've traveled the world through
    And my hair's sparse and grey,
I'd like to go back on that road
    To my old home—to stay.

Beulah H. Ragland

Homecoming

Nostalgia overwhelmed me as I drove up Main Street, made a U-turn, and pulled into the curbless sidewalk in front of the place where I had spent all of my growing-up years. *Place,* not home, for the house had burned down, leaving no trace of its ever having existed.

A ground cover of tall, yellow sunflowers and dripping milkweed obliterated the site. With an increasing sense of despair, I stared at the rank growth until something familiar caught my attention. In the midst of that wilderness our old lilac bush grew in defiant profusion. And twenty feet away the bobbing pink of wild roses nodded over the heads of plate-size sunflowers.

Then, suddenly, I could visualize the old house which had been my home. My heart brimmed over with feeling and a flood of memories engulfed me.

The lilac bush had all but hid the north bedroom. Through the open window, the sweet scent of purple blooms wafted on a gentle summer breeze. With the fragrance came the restful sound of rushing water and rustling cottonwood leaves from the riverbottom behind the house. There was a wedge of star-dappled sky between the lilac bush and a corner of the front porch.

The broad, covered porch ran the length of the living room across the front of the house. There, shaded from the hot afternoon sun, my mother rocked. Long after I'd grown too big to be rocked to sleep,

golden thought

Where there is room in the heart there is always room in the house.

Sir Thomas Moore

golden scripture

But our homeland is that of our Saviour the Lord Jesus Christ in heaven.

Philippians 3:20

the pleasant rhythmic creaking of that old chair induced a feeling of well-being, significant of the love and security I'd found in my mother's cradling arms.

The sweet, wild rose hugged the porch and encompassed the lean-to addition on the southern end of the main structure. The bush grew with abandon, as tall as the roof, a camouflage to cover an ugly but necessary appendage.

An aura of quiet, contented summer surrounded the old house. It awoke in the wash of pink and gold sunrise, to the exultant crowing of the red rooster. Then, after a day in the hot sun, the old house settled creakily into the cool comfort of the long, soft twilight of evening, when the sound of croaking frogs blended with the baaing of sheep and the distant barking of a dog. Summer, without problems or worries or struggles.

Perhaps the peacefulness of summer was an illusion created by the harsh winters into which it was sandwiched. Shoveling snow, carrying coal, stoking fires. Wishing for summer.

Shying away from the struggles of winter, I became conscious of the mid-summer heat and the tall, yellow sunflowers and drippy milkweed, and the total absence of the humble place I had called home. But the old yearning was gone. I knew, finally, that only houses burn down; homes live in the heart and mind and come forth at one's bidding.

Georgia R. Cameron

Mother

She stands against life's storm with fortitude,
   Her ready smile a blanket for all woe,
The turmoil that churns deep within her heart,
   Is something that her children seldom know,
Her child may be a president or clerk
   Bedecked in laurels or behind cold bars;
The blackest sheep find solace in her fold
   For she is close to sacredness and stars.

She is content with simple little things:
   A potted plant, a card, a hurried call,
She nods and smiles when children rush away,
   As though there were no loneliness at all.

O, let us search deep in our hearts today
And tell her things we feel . . . but seldom say.

Annette Victorin

Mother

For care in childhood's helpless days,
For sleepless nights and anxious days,
For loving help in many ways,
    I love you.

For service rendered without thanks,
For patience toward a child's pranks
For wise reproof—yes, even spanks,
    I love you.

For all the time and care you took
To read me many a worthwhile book
In hours when you your rest forsook,
    I love you.

For opening youth's unheeding eyes
To beauty that around us lies
In field and forest, earth and skies
    I love you.

For many a humble, homely deed,
Performed to meet the family need,
For making "Others first" your creed,
    I love you.

For many an hour of stress and strain,
For cheerfulness in spite of pain,
For counting work for others, gain,
    I love you.

For all these things, and others too,
Your daily gifts a long life through,
But most of all, because you're you,
    I love you.

N. O. Moore

The Living Masterpiece

No masterpiece you painted
    On ceilings high in Rome,
But both your boys remember
    You lived one in your home.

You penned no epic poem
    That critics might call art,
But with a grander vision,
    You wrote one in your heart.

You carved no Parian marble
    In sculptured Greek design,
But with your loving fingers
    You shaped this life of mine.

You built no white cathedral
    By echoed footsteps trod,
But in simple faith you made
    Our home a house of God.

Not the hand of Raphael
    Or Michelangelo
Could paint Mother as she is—
    Only her children know.

H. M. S. Richards

Treasures

I treasure most the simple things
That fill my life with rich content:
The little tasks that must be done
At home before the day is spent.

I love the path my neighbor made
Across the grass up to my door;
My lawn that once was smoothly green
Is now much dearer than before.

When dusky twilight shadows fall,
I hold so dear my glowing light,
Sweet melodies I hear, and bed
With cool, clean sheets all shining white.

It is so very clear to me
I have no need to seek afar
Beyond my door for happiness,
For here at home the treasures are!

William Arnette Wofford

A Bridge Instead Of A Wall

They say a wife and husband, bit by bit,
Can rear between their lives a mighty wall,
So thick they can not talk with ease through it,
Nor can they see across, it stands so tall!
Its nearness frightens them but each alone
Is powerless to tear its bulk away,
And each, dejected, wishes he had known
For such a wall, some magic thing to say.

So let us build with master art, my dear,
A bridge of faith between your life and mine,
A bridge of tenderness and very near
A bridge of understanding, strong and fine—
Till we have formed so many lovely ties
There never will be room for walls to rise!

Author Unknown

44

golden thought

A man must first govern himself ere he is fit to govern a family; and his family ere he is fit to bear the government of the commonwealth.

Sir Walter Raleigh

What Is A Dad?

A dad is a person you can always rely upon to be strong.

A dad is strength and steadiness. Like a sturdy oak he stands, sheltering his growing family from the storms and adverse winds of life.

A dad is the person who always knows that time is a great leveler. He has the patience, born of experience, that takes the long view and sees the sun shining beyond the present storm.

A dad is the person you go to when you know you will get a straight answer. He never glosses things over or coats them with sugar, but will always tell you the facts.

A dad is a person who always has a sage bit of wit or wisdom for any situation, drawn from the wealth of his experience and acquaintance.

A dad is the person who can turn a seeming calamity into a smile by turning the light side up.

A dad is the person who earns and deserves the title head of the house. It is his judgment and foresight that safely steers the home ship through the years.

A dad is a person who talks less about love than he shows it. His love is always there, evident in the dust in his face when he comes home at night, the sweat on his brow, and the strong hands that are continually working for his family.

A dad is the person who sets the example his children most want to emulate. His industry, devotion and care are the heritage his sons and daughters carry with them throughout their lives.

A dad is the reason that sons are proud to have sons who will proudly carry the name he has blessed.

Roger L. Kerr

Dad And Me Together

I often think of days gone by,
Back when I was a lad,
Of how I always loved to be,
A taggin' 'round with Dad.
He taught me by example things,
That time and age can't sever,
And many happy times we've had
    Dad and me together.

I remember once, 'twas long ago,
While walking down the lane,
The birds were singing, here and there,
Each one its own refrain.
Dad told me that old adage,
About the birds, "birds of a feather,"
And I kept thinking while we walked,
    Dad and me together.

The years passed by and changes came,
With a family of my own,
We many times went back again,
To that old country home.
Dad's steps were slow and shorter now,
But still it seemed he'd rather,
And soon we'd be a walkin' 'round,
    Dad and me together.

Dad's gone now, he's left us here,
Lonesome, sad at heart,
And yet we knew the time would come,
Someday we'd have to part.
But if I, like Dad, can sail life's sea,
Through rough and stormy weather,
There'll come a time, we'll be again,
    Dad and me together.

Ottis Shirk

Bless Him, O Lord

Mender of toys, leader of boys,
Changer of fuses, kisser of bruises,
Bless him, dear Lord.

Wiper of noses, pruner of roses,
Singer of songs, righter of wrongs,
Bless him, O Lord.

Mover of couches, soother of ouches,
Pounder of nails, teller of tales,
Reward him, O Lord.

Hanger of screens, counsellor of teens,
Fixer of bikes, chastiser of tykes,
Help him, O Lord.

Raker of leaves, cleaner of eaves,
Dryer of dishes, fulfiller of wishes,
Guard him, O Lord.

Changer of tires, builder of fires,
Beloved end of all my desires,
Bless him, O Lord.

Author Unknown

Parents

Standing by the crib of one's own baby, with that world-old pang of compassion and protectiveness toward this so little creature that has all its course to run, the heart flies back in yearning and gratitude to those who felt just so toward one's self.

Then for the first time one understands the homely succession of sacrifices and pains by which life is transmitted and fostered down the stumbling generations of men.

Christopher Morley

Father's Birthday Picnic

This picnic was a special time
For father's friends to meet
Beneath the shade of mighty oaks
Green velvet under feet.

Each year the brothers, cousins, aunts
And children by the score
Would gather like migrating birds
On Maryland's western shore.

Dad loved his proud ancestral home
His friends and family,
The groaning board of meats and fruits;
The laughter—joyous, free.

He held to old traditions like
Blue candles on his cake,
And songs one sings at birthday time
For old, best friendship's sake.

A decade now has passed us by—
No more the happy ring
Of quoits that hit the stake, nor sight
Of children on the swing.

No more the meeting of the clan—
No more news we hear,
Yet memory's photo album brings
Recall of days held dear.

Katherine Paxson

48

Our Little Boy

Cap askew, hair out of place,
Laughing, freckled, dirty face;
Out of bed at break of day,
A little food—a lot of play;
Whistling as he goes his way,
    That's our little boy:

Speeding on his battered bike,
Always on a ride or hike;
Rushing in for ball and bat,
Western guns and lariat;
Wrestler, monkey, acrobat,
    That's our little boy:

Part-time angel, part-time clown,
Dancing eyes of deepest brown;
Pajama-clad on bended knee,
Saying prayers so reverently. . . .
    That's our little boy!

Dorothy M. Cahoon

Hidden Treasures

Marbles, gum and rusty nails,
A little boat that once had sails;
Worms and stones, old wood and string,
Odds and ends of everything;
Treasures that bring endless joy
To the heart of little boy,
Hidden deep 'til mother cleans
The pockets of his faded jeans.

Dorothy M. Cahoon

Let's Read It Together
the children's corner

How God Made Kittens

I think I know how God made you
With your little elfin face:
He took a tiny pansy
That bloomed with special grace,
And added twelve white whiskers,
Two lovely topaz eyes,
An extra touch of velvet
For some small child's surprise;
He took some little stickers
From a wee, wild baby rose,
And made some teeny mittens
And a tiny wet, pink nose,
A bit of love and beauty,
Some playful, soft allure,
Then hid inside a purr-box,
Filled to the brim with purr!
A little bell of silver
He gave for your meow—
"I'll give the world a kitten
To go with its bow-wow,"
He said; "I've made a doggie,
Kids need a kitten, too,"—
And so God gave to children
The precious gift—of you!

Louise Weibert Sutton

Sandy's Unhappy Birthday

Why did we have to move three days before my birthday, thought Sandy as she set the table for dinner. This is the worst birthday I've ever had. Mom and Dad have been busy unpacking all day. And I don't know a single person in this neighborhood. There's no one to play with.

Even her dog, Bluebell, wasn't being any fun. The small terrier lay sleeping in the corner. She had been sleeping most of the day. Mother said that Bluebell needed lots of rest because her puppies would be born soon, but Sandy wished her dog would run and play with her.

"Come on," said Sandy, opening the screen door.

But the dog just sat there.

"Come on, Bluebell. Let's go."

But Bluebell wouldn't move.

"My goodness, do I have to carry you?" said Sandy, letting the door close. She walked over to the dog, picked her up, and carried her out to the yard.

"There," said Sandy, putting Bluebell down on the patio. "Boy, you sure are acting funny today. Now let's take a walk."

Sandy led the way past the porch swing, the lemon tree, and the pink and purple flowers.

Sandy looked around.

There, peeping over the stone wall from the yard next door, was a boy.

"Hi," he said. "My name is Paul. That's a nice dog you've got there. I wish I had a dog."

"What have you got?" asked Sandy.

"Fish. I have a big tank full of fish. But I wish I had a dog."

Just then Sandy's mother came to the screen door. "Time for dinner," she called.

"Well, so long," said Paul.

"Good-bye," said Sandy, heading for the house. The food smelled so good that she didn't notice whether Bluebell was following along.

Mother had all of Sandy's favorites for dinner—macaroni and cheese, pickles, fried chicken, and biscuits with honey. Dessert was a chocolate birthday cake with fluffy marshmallow frosting.

"Make a wish," said Sandy's daddy, lighting the eight pink candles and the red one to grow on.

Sandy closed her eyes and wished that something nice would happen to make this a happy birthday. Then she blew out all the candles with one breath.

Continued on page 52

Continued from page 51

Mother served the cake. As Sandy ate the last bit of frosting on her plate she looked down, thinking that Bluebell would be waiting for a taste.

Where is that dog, thought Sandy. She sure is acting strange today. This is the first time she's ever stayed away from the dinner table. Something must be wrong.

Sandy went into her room and looked under the bed. No dog. She looked out the window at the backyard. Maybe Bluebell had stayed out there. But the dog was nowhere to be seen.

Suddenly, Sandy remembered Paul. He wanted a dog so badly. Could he have sneaked over the wall and taken Bluebell while Sandy was eating dinner? She had to find out.

Sandy hurried out of her room. Maybe Paul had tied Bluebell up in his yard. Just as Sandy was about to dash through the laundry room on her way to the screen door, she stopped short. There, lying on a pile of sheets and towels, was Bluebell. And there beside her was a tiny black puppy.

"Oh, Bluebell. You've had a baby," said Sandy, kneeling down. "You had your baby on my birthday. Paul didn't take you after all."

Sandy touched the warm, wiggling puppy. It was so small that it could have fit into Sandy's hand with room to spare. Sandy had never seen anything so wonderful in her whole life.

She ran into the dining room where her parents were still drinking coffee.

"Mommy! Daddy!" she shouted. "Guess what? Bluebell's had a puppy."

"Now you'll have two dogs," said her father.

"I'd love to keep the puppy," said Sandy, "but maybe I should give it to Paul instead. He's the boy who lives next door and he has no dog at all."

"Why, that's a lovely idea," said Mother. "What a nice friend you are. Let's see the puppy."

Sandy led the way into the laundry room. Bluebell was lying on her bed of sheets and towels and there against her was not one puppy, but two.

"Now I can have a puppy, too," said Sandy. "There's one for me and one for Paul."

She touched the two furry black balls. Their eyes were tightly shut.

"I'm going to call my puppy Happy," said Sandy, "because this is the happiest birthday I ever had."

Susan Goldman

Hawaii

Daily Life

do not be anxious about tomorrow for tomorrow will have anxieties of its own.

matthew 6:34

If You Really Want To Make It!

If you really want to make it then you have to start from scratch,
Ignoring little grievances that petty people hatch.
You have to keep your temper or you'll never get ahead,
How many times we've spoken words we never should have said.
There is no man so mighty that he can stand alone,
The greatest fool would never try to make it on his own.
What sweetness lies within you, but you have to bring it out,
Loving—Sharing—Caring—that's what life is all about.

If you really want to make it you must proceed with care,
Stumbling not along the paths that angels never dare.
Keeping faith with precepts far wiser than your own,
Building something lasting though your name is never known.
Finding satisfaction in whatever you may do,
Staunchly persevering until the job is through.
Finding strength to meet demands that only you can fill,
Let clouds hide the sun from view and rain fall where it will!

If you really want to make it you'll have to learn to be
As forgiving and as patient as the Lord has been with thee.
There is no man among us so perfect he can claim
Immunity from error and innocence from blame.
You'll get no special privileges whatever your degree,
Without a credit in the course of basic charity.
However great your fortune—you cannot buy ONE DAY,
So live your life remembering you are not here to stay!

Grace E. Easley

golden Scripture

And why take ye thought for raiment? Consider the lilies of the field, how they grow; they toil not, neither do they spin:

And yet I say unto you, That even Solomon in all his glory was not arrayed like one of these.

Wherefore, if God so clothe the grass of the field, which today is, and tomorrow is cast into the oven, shall he not much more clothe you, O ye of little faith?

Therefore take no thought, saying, What shall we eat? or, What shall we drink? or, Wherewithal shall we be clothed?

(For after all these things do the Gentiles seek:) for your heavenly Father knoweth that ye have need of all these things.

But seek ye first the kingdom of God, and his righteousness; and all these things shall be added unto you.

Matthew 6:28-33

It Takes Courage

It takes courage to smile when the world is dark
And the sun just refuses to shine,
When you've lost your way and your heart is sad
And the path is an upward climb.

It takes courage to hope when your hope is gone
And nothing just seems to be right,
Today just an echo of yesterdays gone
With naught but the darkness of night.

It takes courage to dream when your mind is adrift
And a weariness enters your soul . . .
When you long for contentment and peace in your heart
But can't seem to conquer your goal.

It takes courage to smile, it takes courage to hope . . .
A courage when all else is gone,
When clouds overshadow the sun in your sky,
It takes courage to smile and go on.

Garnett Ann Schultz

I've Never Sailed
The Seven Seas

I've never sailed the Seven Seas,
But I have stood within the gentle curve
Of Portage Bay at close of day,
Watching the great tides move and sway.
     And so I love the sea.

I've never climbed the mighty Alps,
But just beyond the foothills of my town,
With sunset glow or storms upon its crown,
Stands Baker, great White Watcher, looking down.
     And so I love the mountain heights.

I've never worshipped in a temple dim,
Or listened to the bells on altars far,
But I have knelt within a humble place,
Have felt the presence of God's blessed grace.
     And so I love each dedicated place.

So now, though home, I've seen and sensed
In miniature, the wonderment of distant scene.
Such dear familiar things—might it not be—
Bring time and space and beauty close to me?
     And so my glad heart sings.

Sue Boynton

WE live in deeds, not years;
In thoughts, not breath;
In feelings, not in figures on the dial.

We should count time
By heart-throbs when they beat
For God, for man, for duty.

He most lives
Who thinks most,
Feels noblest, acts the best.

Philip James Bailey

GOLDEN PRAYER

Slow Me Down Lord

If I go down the road too fast
And fail to see a brother walking past,
Or miss small pleasures every day;
Nor see a blessing fall my way—
Then slow me down Lord, so that I
Might see an angel passing by.
Slow me down, that I may talk
With You Lord. Slow me to a walk.

Lucille Crumley

A Light Shining In The Darkness

One evening on a hike along a country road, someone noticed a tiny speck of light in an adjoining meadow. It was smaller than the reflection of the tiniest star on a surface of water. The light disappeared in a moment, but others appeared intermittently.

An amateur naturalist explained that the light came from the glow-worm. He picked up one for inspection. It was a very small insect, emitting a light so feeble that it would be noticed only on a dark night.

In the great meadow of life there are people of whose presence we are not conscious until in some hour of darkness we see from those insignificant lives an unexpected glow of courage, faith, neighborliness, friendliness, devotion, or love. A lowly private in a losing battle performs an heroic act which turns the tide; a young man makes a home for his orphaned brothers and sisters.

A tiny glow from one life in darkness is worth a thousand of those who can sparkle only in the sunshine of prosperity and well-being.

The American Way

There's No View

After three weeks of near-fatal illness in a hospital I was allowed to sit up, and a nurse wheeled me over to a window.

"There's no view," she said apologetically. "Just a dingy courtyard."

It was a narrow stone enclosure darkening with dusk. I saw the top of a parked ambulance; a row of garbage cans; a cat, tail high, silhouetted against the fading light; the tarnished leaves of an ailanthus tree, rooted in cement.

From her viewpoint the view *was* dingy. But to me, after my brush with death, it was achingly beautiful. I promised myself, passionately, that I never again would take such things as the grace of a cat or the symmetry of a tree for granted.

Of course, once I was back home in my normal routine, I couldn't hold on to the depth of sensation I felt then. But I have learned that by making a conscious effort it is possible to keep the mind and heart alive to the daily wonders of life.

Elizabeth Byrd

GOLDEN THOUGHTS

I steer my bark with Hope ahead and Fear astern.

Thomas Jefferson

'Tis the mind that makes the body rich.

William Shakespeare

God's love for poor sinners is very wonderful, but God's patience with ill-natured saints is a deeper mystery.

Henry Drummond

The Sounion Is Sinking

We had looked forward to our trip to the Holy Land, never dreaming it would take us into the most terrifying experience of our lives.

Esther and I were in our 70's. I had just retired from my job as a rural mail carrier and our plans were to sell our small farm to one of the grandchildren and move into a retirement home.

But we had always longed to visit the land where Jesus walked and when our pastor, Joe Timberlake, approached us about joining a tour group going to Israel, we decided it was now or never.

In February, 1973, we joined 250 others, most of whom were about our age, and flew to Cyprus, where we boarded the passenger ship MTV Sounion. Esther and I were assigned a tiny cabin on the second deck. It had a double-decked bunk which we didn't like, but we decided to make the best of it. After sailing on the Mediterranean to Tarsus, St. Paul's home town, we docked in Beirut, Lebanon.

The fact that we were headed for Israel caused some of our group to wonder if the Palestinian terrorist group, Black September, might try to harm us. However, such thoughts were soon lost in the thrill of seeing places we had read about all our lives.

After a day of sightseeing in Beirut, Esther and I returned to the ship. We ate a quick supper and, because of Esther's bad heart condition, retired early to our cabin. The ship was to leave the harbor at 1:30 a.m. and, like most of the passengers, we wanted to go to bed early so we could rise at dawn and see the sun coming up over the Holy Land at Haifa.

I was thankful our cabin was next to the dock because the lights of Beirut shone through the thick glass of the small, sealed porthole, giving our cabin a cozy feeling. I reached down, touched Esther's extended hand, breathed a quiet prayer of thanksgiving for what tomorrow held, and drifted off to sleep.

Suddenly, a tremendous explosion rocked the ship, jolting me awake. Whistles and horns began shrieking. Dazed, I clambered down and turned on the light. Esther had been thrown to the floor.

The lights flickered and went out, leaving us in blackness. The whistles and horns stopped, and we felt the ship begin to lean.

"We've been bombed!" Esther screamed. "We're sinking!"

I grabbed the stateroom door. But the twisting effect of the explosion had jammed it tight.

We were trapped. Cold water was surging in under the door and rising rapidly in the stateroom.

I released the door and grappled in the dark for Esther. The lights of the city no longer reflected in our cabin as the ship continued to list farther away from the dock.

The water was up to our knees. Esther was almost hysterical; I held her close to calm her.

The floor continued to tilt and the only sound in the inky blackness was the surge of rising water and Esther's sobs.

"We're going to die, aren't we?" Esther sobbed.

I knew we were in danger of capsizing. I also knew there could be another explosion as the water reached the ship's boilers. Yet I dared not frighten Esther with such thoughts. Instead, I remembered the scripture I had read the day before we left. "When thou passest through the waters, I will be with thee; and through the rivers, they shall not overflow thee."

I began to pray out loud, thanking God for His deliverance. The moment I finished, she took up the prayer of thanksgiving also. In that black moment on the sinking ship, sharing our prayers and praising God together drew us closer than we had ever been.

The luminous dial of my watch said 10:45. We had been trapped almost half an hour. There was no sound of help from the outside.

Unable to stand on the slanting floor, we had to brace ourselves against the wall. The cold, oily water rose to my chest and then to my chin. Now I had to lift Esther to keep her head above it.

And then the water seemed to stop rising. But for how long?

Now another danger. Esther and I were rapidly using up the oxygen in the small amount of air left to us. I struggled to the porthole and tried to break the glass. It was much too thick and I knew the steel hull was at least an inch thick. I slipped back down, urging Esther to relax while I held her head out of water. I knew that with her bad heart she could not stand much more.

We prayed. Waited. Listened. And prayed some more.

Our clothes, the expensive camera we bought for the trip, the souvenirs were all lost somewhere under the dark water. But they were of no concern. Only our lives counted now. An hour and a half passed. We could not last much longer.

Everyone else on the ship had safely escaped, and the ship's captain was making plans to get the passengers into hotels.

Only our pastor, Joe Timberlake, objected. He had been frantically searching for us and was now convinced we were trapped in our cabin. The captain, irritated over Joe's demands to check the ship, suggested that we had not returned to it.

Finally the captain agreed to send a crew member into the hull to shine a light into our porthole to prove the stateroom was empty.

Down in our water-filled cabin I knew our oxygen was almost gone. We prayed aloud once more. When we slipped below the surface, I wanted our last words to be ones of praise to our Heavenly Father.

Continued on page 62

Continued from page 61

Suddenly a light flashed through the porthole. Releasing Esther to cling to that top bunk, I crawled to it and waved my hand under the glass. "Air," I croaked, knowing I could not be heard.

But God heard, and moments later a sledgehammer smashed the porthole. Slivers of glass showered us, but with them came a wonderful rush of fresh air.

Moments later Joe Timberlake's anxious face appeared in the tiny window. The captain had asked him to comfort us while they prepared an acetylene torch to cut through the ship.

Then another face appeared. It was Russell Bennett, a young garage mechanic. He had come on the tour because he felt God had a special purpose for his life. He had seen that the Lebanese dock worker could not operate the torch. An expert welder, Russ leaped onto the side of the ship and grabbed the torch. Moments later the intense flame was eating into the steel plates.

But as the flame broke through, white-hot molten steel peppered us. Esther screamed in pain and I cried out, "We're being roasted!"

"Get down in the water as low as you can," Russell shouted. "We'll spray you with a hose and I'll try to deflect the flame."

They sprayed cold water on my head and back. A shaking chill convulsed me as I hung to the top bunk, holding Esther. My grip weakened as nausea flooded me and I feared I might lose my semiconscious wife into the water. I prayed again and the convulsion stopped.

It took 20 minutes to cut an 18-inch hole in the side of the ship. I pushed Esther's nearly lifeless body up and minutes later I was also lifted out. An ambulance rushed us to the hospital. Esther's heart had almost stopped beating and she was placed in intensive care.

Thank God Esther recovered. Our Holy Land tour was cut short but we had already found the revelation that no sightseeing trip could have ever given us. Esther and I are now able to praise God for our difficulties that night. That top bunk, for instance, saved our lives. And the jammed door. If we had gone into the dark passageway, we would have surely become lost in the bowels of that sinking ship.

Our lives have been much different since we've returned home. For one thing, material possessions no longer occupy first place in our lives. We learned how meaningless they really are.

Neither am I looking at tomorrow for our blessings. That night in Beirut, we thought our greatest blessing would come when we set foot on the Holy Land the next day. Now I understand the full truth of Jesus's statement, "Don't be anxious about tomorrow . . . Live one day at a time."

If we let Him, He will bless us today, even in our times of despair.

Philip Griffin

Familiarity

Those who live by the sea
Too familiar grow
With the changing ways of it,
And its magic ebb and flow.
Nothing they see or care to know
Save when the tide be high or low.

Though green waves glitter
With white flung spray
By their kitchen fires
They bend all day
They turn their backs on the
   selfsame sea
That can make the heart leap up
   in me!

Rachel Field

What Is Happiness?

Happiness is to have enough for each day's needs and something left to share with those who have not. It is to possess the love of friends and to bring them joy. It is to love and be loved.

Happiness is to have some worthwhile task to do, however small, and the courage with which to meet life's challenges. It is to cherish the gift of laughter and to see truth and beauty in all things.

Happiness is to be content with one's fortune and to live in peace with all mankind.

Barbara Burrow

gOldEN NUGGET

This above all: to thine own self be true,
And it must follow, as the night the day,
Thou canst not then be false to any man.

William Shakespeare

Follow The Gleam

Not of the sunlight,
Not of the moonlight,
Not of the starlight,
O young Mariner,
Down to the haven.
Call your companions,
Launch your vessel,
And crowd your canvas,
And, ere it vanishes
Over the margin.
After, follow it,
Follow the Gleam.

Alfred Tennyson

On The North Side Of The Tree

It is said that when Stradivarius went out to get wood to make his famous violins, he chose the north side of the tree because it had withstood wind and storm and had thereby gained strength that produced the sweetest music.

Nobody likes bearing the brunt of trouble. But to do so with strength and resilience is to become stronger and sweeter in character. Remember this when you find yourself on that cold, unsheltered north side of life.

Esther York Burkholder

64

Pass It On

Have you had a kindness shown?
   Pass it on.
'Twas not given for thee alone,
   Pass it on.
Let it travel down the years,
Let it wipe another's tears,
'Til in heav'n the deed appears—
   Pass it on.

Did you hear the loving word?
   Pass it on—
Like the singing of a bird?
   Pass it on.
Let its music live and grow,
Let it cheer another's woe;
You have reaped what others sow—
   Pass it on.

'Twas the sunshine of a smile—
   Pass it on.
Staying but a little while!
   Pass it on.
April beam a little thing,
Still it wakes the flowers of spring,
Makes the silent birds to sing—
   Pass it on.

Have you found the heavenly light?
   Pass it on.
Souls are groping in the night,
   Daylight gone—
Hold thy lighted lamp on high,
Be a star in someone's sky,
He may live who else would die—
   Pass it on.

Be not selfish in thy greed,
   Pass it on.
Look upon thy brother's need,
   Pass it on.
Live for self, you live in vain;
Live for Christ, you live again;
Live for Him, with Him you reign—
   Pass it on.

Henry Burton, 1840–1930

Along Our Way

The canopy of azure sky
Looked down this carefree day—
On great tall trees and winding trails
We saw along our way.
The chuckle of the stream was heard,
All silvery with joy—
Because there waded in its midst
A little girl and boy.
The luring scent of stately pine
Drew us into a glade,
And there we glimpsed a startled fawn;
Sun dappled in the shade.
The forest is a kindly place
Where flowers nod and smile;
The songbirds, perched on branches high,
Sang for us all the while.
Along our way we found these scenes,
Like paintings rich and rare;
To God, Creator of it all—
We gave our thanks in prayer.

Esther B. Heins

I Can

So high is grandeur to our dead,
So near is God to man,
Where Duty whispers low, *Thou must,*
The youth replies, *I can.*

Ralph Waldo Emerson

A Good Memory Lesson

Forget each kindness that you do
    As soon as you have done it;
Forget the praise that falls to you
    The moment you have won it;
Forget the slander that you hear
    Before you can repeat it;
Forget each slight, each spite, each sneer
    Wherever you may meet it.

Remember kindness that is done
    To you whate'er its measure;
Remember praise by others won
    And pass it on with pleasure;
Remember every promise made
    And keep it to the letter;
Remember those who lend you aid
    And be a grateful debtor.

Remember all the happiness
    That comes your way in living;
Forget each worry and distress,
    Be hopeful and forgiving;
Remember good, remember truth,
    Remember heaven's above you;
And you will find, through age and youth,
    That many hearts will love you.

Heywood Skinner

These Little Things

Such little things make life more sweet,
A child's bright smile across the street,
A letter from a far-off friend,
A woodland lane that has no end;
A berry bush, tall, swaying corn,
A spindly calf, just newly-born,
The fumes of spicy apple pie,
Small winking stars up in the sky;
A little dog's deep faith in me,
White sails unfurled against the sea;
The pressure of a kind, warm hand,
A few close friends who understand.
Such little things make each day shine,
What others vainly search, is mine.

Annette Victorin

Ups And Downs

When things go wrong, as they
    sometimes will,
And you feel you're facing a long,
    steep hill,
Just settle down and start to climb;
Take it one-step-at-a-time.

Don't fret about how long the
    road,
How tired you are, how big the
    load,
Just keep your eyes upon the top,
Plod along and never stop,
And when you reach the peak,
    you'll thrill
That just ahead *it's all downhill!*

Martin Buxbaum

LET'S READ IT TOGETHER
the children's corner

An Eskimo Grocery Store

Sometimes it's fun to go to the grocery store with your mother. But how would you like it if your mother also invited your father and all your sisters and brothers, your grandparents, all your cousins and aunts and uncles, and all the people in your neighborhood? Of course, she wouldn't do that. But there's an island in Alaska where over 300 people in a village go to the grocery store at the same time.

These people are Eskimos and live in the village of Savoonga on St. Lawrence Island. Their island in the Bering Sea is only 38 miles from the coast of Russia. When the sky is clear, they can see Russia's mountains across the water.

In the winter, while the men are hunting walrus and seal, the children attend village school. In the summer, when school is out, they hike over the hills, ride with their parents in *umiaks* (skinboats, much like canoes), or climb the cliff rocks to look for birds. But the most fun of all is in July when everyone goes to the grocery store at the same time.

Once a year the "North Star," a supply boat from Seattle, comes to St. Lawrence Island and anchors about a mile offshore. Everyone goes down to the beach and waits for the first barge to land, bringing coal, flour, salt, and boxes and boxes of canned goods. Everyone works to unload the supplies and to carry them up the beach to the village store, the schoolhouse, and the church. The children watch for small boxes that look about the right size for candy bars.

Two barges go back and forth between the "North Star" and the beach until all the supplies for Savoonga have been brought to shore. Everything must be unloaded quickly because the "North Star" carries supplies for other villages, too, and must reach them all before ice begins to form on the ocean.

Some of the men and women work all day and all the next day to finish unloading. But when the children get tired of helping, they climb up on the oil drums and play tag. When they catch someone, they shout *alungik* (you're it)! After awhile they go home to bed.

When all the boxes, sacks, and oil drums are off the beach and stored neatly away, ladies begin coming to the little village store to buy groceries for their families. The children come looking for candy bars. Because sweets are so rare on St. Lawrence Island, the supply of candy will only last about a week, but many of the other groceries will have to last until the "North Star" returns again the next July.

Carole Charles

Work And Play

Work and Play by chance one day
Met and talked along the way.
And as people will who chat
Fell to arguing this and that
"Which of us," said Play, "think you
Is the better of the two?"

"Well," said Work, "look 'round about.
See the dreams that I've worked out.
See the gardens I have made.
See the pavements I have laid.
See the wonders I have wrought
And the homes I've built and bought."

"Yes," said Play, "that's very true,
But no man is fond of you,
I'm the one they most desire,
I'm their laughter 'round the fire,
I'm the songs they sing, and I
Am the twinkle in the eye."

"True," said Work, "but I'm their bread,
I'm the blankets on the bed,
I am everything they need,
I supply the books they read,
You, when all is said and done,
Are their merriment and fun."

Came a gray old sage who smiled,
"Boys," said he, "be reconciled.
You are partners—hand in hand.
Side by side you two must stand.
Wise men always give the day
First to work and then to play."

Edgar A. Guest

American Heritage

Blessed is the nation whose God is the Lord; and the people whom he hath chosen for his own inheritance.

What Is America?

It's the dream of billions of dreamers
Grown of seeds they have sown—
A symbol of hope for the future
Purchased in blood of their own.

It is more than a number of boundaries
And rivers so deep and so long;
It's a fortress blocking the pathway,
A barrier built against wrong.

It's more than its snow-capped mountains
And shores where the waves dash high;
It's a kerchief to dry up the tear drops,
A solace for those who cry.

It's more than its well-lighted cities
And its hustle and bustle by day;
It's the hope of the suffering masses
And the answer to those who pray.

It's more than a single great nation
With a Star Spangled Banner unfurled;
It's the rock that was planned at creation,
It's the hope of the whole wide world.

Sergeant Clement L. Lockwood

GOldEN pRAYER

Almighty God of my Fathers,
Give me the courage to stand
And speak the truth I know, to friend and foe,
And to walk with my brothers, hand in hand.
Help me to see clearly, Father,
What you would have me do,
Give me the strength for the task,
That's all I ask—to honor the Red, White and Blue.
Restore a right spirit within my heart,
To want for every man, liberty,
And when I see oppression, help me do my part
To right the wrong, and bring harmony.
Almighty God of my Fathers,
Humbly I come; hear my plea—
Give us the grace to see
Truth and Liberty go hand in hand
In a land that is free!

Dale Evans Rogers

All Praise Be Unto Thee!

Not unto us, not unto us—
    All praise be unto Thee!
For all the gold our coffers hold
    Is Thine, from sea to sea.

Not unto us the glory, Lord,
    For power on sea and land.
Thine be the praise, who set our ways,
    Who guideth with Thy hand.

Not unto us the laurel crown,
    Though name and fame be ours.
Without Thy aid all lowly laid
    Would be our vaunted powers.

Not unto us, not unto us!
    Upon Thy will we wait.
Through all the days Thy Name we raise
    Who made our nation great.

Arthur Gordon Field

George Washington

The Commander in Chief was reconnoitering near White Plains, N.Y., when a courier dashed up, crying: "The British are on the camp, Sir!" The general galloped full tilt back to camp, where he was told that his outposts had been beaten in. He turned to his officers. "Gentlemen," said George Washington, "you will repair to your respective posts and do the best you can."

George Washington always did the best he could—and it was enough to create and sustain a nation. Perhaps he provided the key to his own achievements. "We ought not to look back," he once wrote, "unless it is to derive useful lessons from past errors."

His learning was hard-earned. His father, big "Gus" Washington, a Virginia land speculator and iron-mine owner, died when George was eleven, leaving him with a querulous mother whom he spent much of his life trying to avoid. He had less formal education than any other early American President, picking up enough math to get started as a surveyor and painstakingly copying 110 "Rules of Civility and Decent Behavior." Samples: "Cleanse not your teeth with the tablecloth," and "Labor to keep alive in your breast that little spark of celestial fire called conscience."

There is something not quite pleasant about the young Washington. As a soldier rising to colonel in Virginia's militia, he was forever squabbling with British authorities about "honor" and "preferment," which seemed synonymous in his mind. He was less than modest: "I can truly say and confidently assert that no soldiers were ever under better command," he said, speaking of his own men. But he was also—and always—brave. After his first battle, in which he defeated a French force near Fort Duquesne in the Western wilderness, he reported: "I heard the bullets whistle, and, believe me, there is something charming in the sound." During the woodlands massacre of Britain's General Edward Braddock and his forces, Washington had two horses shot from beneath him, his coat shredded by bullets that not only whistled but pierced. Years later, as the American Commander in Chief at Princeton, he rode to within 30 yards of the British line and (as an aide covered his own face with his hat so as not to see what must surely happen) survived the crossfire between enemy troops and his own.

In 1758, at age 26, he left military service and settled into Mount Vernon, the family estate on the Potomac. There he spent the next 17 years of his life, and there he may be caught in the cameo of repose. By the standards of his day he was immense, standing, as he described himself, "6 ft. high" (though after his death his secretary measured him

Continued on page 76

Continued from page 75

at 6 ft. 3½ in.), weighing nearly 200 lbs., with huge hands and feet (size 13 boots), chestnut hair and light smallpox scars on the end of his nose. He married 27-year-old Martha Custis, one of the wealthiest widows in America (her inheritance was reckoned at £23,632), who was barely 5 ft. tall and, whenever she wished to speak to him, had to pluck at his coat buttons for attention. Besides farming, Washington served quietly but effectively in the Virginia House of Burgesses where, as a member named Thomas Jefferson noted, he was "in action cool, like a bishop at his prayers."

As his long sojourn neared its end, he was elected to the Continental Congress in Philadelphia, and there, because he was the most experienced officer from a militarily and politically strategic state, he was unanimously named head of the revolutionary army. The date: June 15, 1775.

On the eve of command Washington wrote: "I am now embarked on a tempestuous ocean, from whence perhaps, no friendly harbor is to be found." Not many privies were to be found either in the Continental encampments outside Boston, and one of Washington's first acts was to protest that shortage. It was, for him, too often that kind of niggling war. But he learned as he went along, and on the bloodstained road that led to Yorktown, he made some major discoveries: this war went by no Old World book; in the American vastness, mere territorial gains meant little; mobility was the key, and even the fleetness of foot which his men often displayed when things went badly could be an advantage —they could run and live to fight another day. Valley Forge was a nadir best described by a member of the Connecticut Line: "Poor food —hard lodging—cold weather—fatigue—nasty clothes—nasty cookery —vomit half my time—smoked out of my senses—the devil's in it— I can't endure it." But Washington made good use even of those grim days: he turned his ragtags over to the Prussian drillmaster Steuben, who made soldiers of them. And finally, unbelievably, it was all over: George Washington was free to return to "the shadow of my own vine and my own fig tree."

But not for long. He watched restively as the frail coalition of former colonies began to fall apart, and when a call came to go to Philadelphia, he was ready. On May 25, 1787, he was unanimously named president of the Constitutional Convention. For four months, he sat on a low dais, taking almost no part in the debate. But it is entirely possible that there would have been no Constitution had it not been for Washington's presence, and it is almost certain that the Constitution would not have taken the form it did had it not been for the expectation that Washington would be the first President. Wrote Pierce Butler, a Maryland delegate: "Many of the members cast their eyes toward General

Washington as President, and shaped their ideas of the powers to be given to a President by their opinions of his virtue." In New York's Federal Hall, on April 30, 1789, after unanimous election, George Washington was sworn in as the first President of the United States.

He was keenly conscious of being the first. "I walk on untrodden ground," he wrote. "There is scarcely any part of my conduct which may not hereafter be drawn into precedent." Thus he set about creating precedents—on everything from Presidential protocol to constitutional meanings. Example: unsure about the requirement that the President have both the "advice" and the "consent" of the Senate on treaties, he appeared before the Senate in person to present a proposed pact with the Creek Indians. After two tedious days of bickering, he left declaring that he would be "damned if he ever went there again." He never did, and to this day Senate advice has taken a back seat to Senate consent.

He was 62, weary and worried about his failing memory when, with great reluctance, he accepted a second term—again by unanimous vote. As at Princeton years before, he was once more caught between hostile firing lines, this time the opposing political forces of Treasury Secretary Alexander Hamilton and Secretary of State Thomas Jefferson. But Washington endured. At the same time, he performed one of his greatest services to his country: in the explosive aftermath of the French Revolution, he insisted that the U.S. remain neutral and unentangled in Europe's wars. Excepting only the twitch that was the War of 1812, Washington's policy remained America's until 1917.

He left office on March 4, 1797, returning to his beloved Mount Vernon. There, on a December morning in 1799, he awakened Martha to say that he was suffering ague, but he refused to let her summon a servant lest, in getting out of bed, she catch cold herself. He continued to sicken, and in his final seconds he felt his own pulse, silently counting to the beat of faint and fading drums.

GOLDEN THOUGHT

Liberty, when it begins to take root, is a plant of rapid growth.

George Washington

Abraham Lincoln

The President's body was too long for the bed, and his feet dangled over the end. His right eye was black. His breathing was swift and shallow, and occasionally he moaned. Mary Todd Lincoln was brought into the room; she stood wordless for a few moments and was led out again. At 7:22:10 on the morning of April 15, 1865, the President's chest heaved, then relaxed and did not move again. Surgeon General Joseph K. Barnes pressed his ear against the chest, straightened, took two silver coins from his vest pocket and placed them upon the President's eyelids. War Secretary Edwin M. Stanton, who was to become the marplot of the succeeding Administration, had been standing at the foot of the bed, hat in hand. "Now," said Stanton, "he belongs to the ages."

Abraham Lincoln had belonged to all humanity, but to no man. To some, he was Honest Abe or Old Abe or Father Abraham. To others, he was the Rail Splitter or the Great Emancipator. To still others, in the rages of his day, he was the Abolition Emperor or the Orangutan at the White House. In 1963, Time Magazine portrayed Lincoln on its cover and wrote: "He was neither a rebel nor a conservative, but a conserver. He was no artist, except in using public language and in using men. His life was an infinitely varied mixture of leading and following, conforming and defying. He could temporize, compromise and maneuver. But he always held to his own vision and met the exacting definition of an individual set down by French Philosopher Georges Bernanos: 'A man who gives himself or refuses himself, but never lends himself.' Above all, Lincoln was an individual in the special double sense that Americans attribute to the word—the common man who is yet uncommon."

His native soil was the dirt floor of the 18 ft.-by-16 ft. log cabin in backwoods Kentucky, where he was born on a bed of cornhusks and bearskins at a time when, far over the horizon, Thomas Jefferson was just winding up his second term as President. His common blood was that of Thomas Lincoln, a carpenter, and of Nancy Hanks Lincoln, the illegitimate daughter of someone later described by Lincoln as "a nobleman so called of Virginia." Lincoln's boyhood and early maturity have become part of American folklore, as familiar (and far more authentic) to every schoolchild as Parson Weems' story of George Washington and the cherry tree, which was, incidentally, one of the works read by the young Lincoln in the glimmering light of his wood-shavings fire. He seemed contradictory. He was the tall teller of droll tales, some of them spun in moments of considerable discouragement. He was the self-taught lawyer who, since he had no files, kept his papers in his hat. He was the brash bumpkin legislator who sauntered across a ballroom and said to Mary Todd, a vivacious girl of good family: "Miss Todd, I want to dance with you in the worst way." He was the reluctant groom backing out of marriage at the last moment, then spending more than a year in deep, almost suicidal gloom.

But more than anything else, he was, in the noblest meaning of the word, a politician—a mediator between individual dreams and human realities, devoted and determined without being dogmatic, a man who could give without bending and bend without breaking. Herein lay his consistency.

Running for the Illinois assembly in 1832, he introduced himself to the electorate by saying, "I am humble Abraham Lincoln." He lost, but won two years later, and it was in the state legislature that Abraham Lincoln declared himself on slavery. The institution, he said, was "founded on both injustice and bad policy." Twenty-three years later, he could note that his original idea was pretty much "the same that it is now."

Lincoln was elected to the U.S. House of Representatives in 1846 and immediately set about demanding that President Polk cite the exact spot on which the first provocation of the Mexican War had taken place; for this, he won from a partisan press the nickname "Spotty" Lincoln. He left Congress after only one term, convinced that he had been a failure and that he was through with politics.

Slavery changed his mind. When he heard that Illinois' Democratic Senator Stephen A. Douglas had proposed the Kansas-Nebraska Bill, which made the extension of slavery into those territories a matter of popular vote, Lincoln hit the stump, offering passion in Peoria: "I hate it because of the monstrous injustice of slavery itself. I hate it because it deprives our republican example of its just influence in the world . . ." He ran unsuccessfully for the U.S. Senate in 1855, and in 1858 received the Senate nomination of the fledgling Republican Party. He laboriously composed his acceptance speech, and one passage received strong criticism from his friends ("A damn fool utterance," said one). But Lincoln delivered it anyway: "A house divided against itself cannot stand. I believe this Government cannot endure permanently half slave and half free." Lincoln challenged Douglas to a series of face-to-face debates—there were seven of them—and although he lost that election the debates propelled Abraham Lincoln onto the national scene, resulting in his nomination for President in 1860.

Abraham Lincoln—Civil War President. Worry followed by anxiety followed by anguish. When troops were slow to arrive for the defense of Washington: "Why don't they come? Why don't they come!" Later: "The bottom is out of the tub. What shall I do?" After Chancellorsville,

Continued on page 80

Continued from page 79

a murderous Union defeat: "My God! My God! What will the country say? What will the country say?" He went through general after general, a litany of failure: McDowell, McClellan, Pope, McClellan again, Burnside, Hooker, Meade. None satisfied his or the nation's needs. He had a political, not a military mind, but he read up on strategy and tactics. He made many mistakes, but he came to know one thing: it was the army of Robert E. Lee, not the piece of real estate that was Richmond, the Confederate capital, that must be destroyed. To this end, he finally chose as his commander in chief Ulysses S. Grant, on the simple premise that "he fights." Grant did the job. With his help, Lincoln was re-elected President in 1864.

Throughout the war, in moments of victory and of defeat, Lincoln could take pride in America's past and find hope for its future. After the turning point at Gettysburg, he spoke at the dedication there of the cemetery for Union war dead. Legend would have it that he dashed off his remarks on the back of an envelope while on the train to the scene. Not so. He worked hard on the talk, writing and revising. But its words are engraved in American history: "Four score and seven years ago . . ."

Abraham Lincoln had always been a lover of such diversions as theater: "I must have a change of some sort or die." And so, only five days after Appomattox, he and Mary Todd Lincoln went to Ford's Theater in Washington to view a performance of *Our American Cousin.* It was there that he became the first U.S. President to be assassinated. His killer, John Wilkes Booth, leaped to the stage crying, *"Sic semper tyrannis."* Little did his enflamed mind understand that he was to bring down the scourge of a vindictive Reconstruction upon the South he loved. For Abraham Lincoln had had in mind an understanding peace aimed at bringing the Union together again. When a Union general had asked the President how he should treat the people of the defeated South, Lincoln replied: "If I were in your place, I'd let 'em up easy, let 'em up easy."

gOldEN THOUGHT

I leave you, hoping that the lamp of liberty will burn in your bosoms, until there no longer be a doubt that all men are created free and equal.

Abraham Lincoln

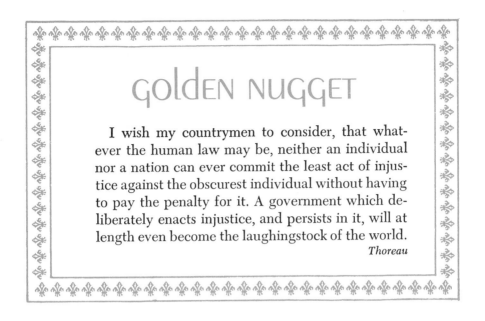

GOLDEN NUGGET

I wish my countrymen to consider, that whatever the human law may be, neither an individual nor a nation can ever commit the least act of injustice against the obscurest individual without having to pay the penalty for it. A government which deliberately enacts injustice, and persists in it, will at length even become the laughingstock of the world.

Thoreau

The Flag Speaks

I am the United States Flag, the symbol of many things.

I am whatever you make me, nothing more, nothing less.

I am the promise of a nation, a mother's dream, a child's desire.

I am your belief in your future, your hope for your family.

I am the flag of many races—white, black, yellow, red.

I am the sweat of a hard day's labor, the thought of a brain, the pain of decision.

I am the Constitution and the statutes, the courts and the legislatures, the voting booth and the soldier, the street sweeper and the executive.

I am compelling reason, a new idea, definition of purpose.

I am earth and sky and sea; I am wind and rain and sun.

I am the right to work and own; the right to play and the right to pray.

I am whatever you make me, nothing more, nothing less.

Author Unknown

This Is America!

Where snow-kissed mountain summits rise,
And eagles soar the morning skies,
Where golden valleys meet the eyes,
—This is America!

Where unmatched cities rise from sod
Long loved by men who honored God,
And far-flung, windy prairies nod,
—This is America!

Where all may say, with freedom still,
Words deepest felt that challenge ill,
And dare to live as free men will,
—This is America!

Where dreams may merge toward hopes more grand,
While courage smiles and values stand,
God bless her noble, sun-arched strand,
—This is America!

Louise Weibert Sutton

Golden Opportunity

Mark Twain was a great writer, lecturer and humorist, but a poor investor. He was always ready to put money into some new and unusual invention. So many "sure-things" failed to work out, however, that Twain finally vowed never to back another inventor as long as he lived.

Shortly after making this momentous decision, Twain was approached by a young man who wanted him to buy stock in his new invention. "Absolutely and positively not," replied Twain, delighted with his new-found willpower. The young man left disappointed. His name was Alexander Graham Bell. He had just invented the telephone.

Author Unknown

Country Store

The faded sign
Through wind and time
Proclaimed our needs
From jugs to lime.

Cheese and crackers
Homemade mittens
Cat in the bean bag
With her kittens.

Buckwheat flour
From the hill
Just ground fresh
At MacKenzie's mill.

Home churned butter
Chewin' 'baccy
Razors, mugs
And strops, b'cracky.

Single trees
Straps to link'em
A brand new salve
And Lydia Pinkum.

Keg molasses
One of pickles
Good barbed wire
And blades for sickles.

Calico
And sorghum pails
Cinnamon
Eight penny nails

Celluloid
And fancy buckles
Kerosine
And Bill Nye chuckles.

Rubber rings
And canning jars
Linement
And taffy bars.

Talcum powder
(Carriage trade)
Doughnuts
That the ladies made.

Gingham bolts
In seven styles
Boys will look
While school girl smiles.

Salted fish
Peppermint sticks
Soda biscuits
Hard rock picks.

But don't you bother 'bout it now
We know your folks and kin.
We'll settle when your man gets well
And when the crops come in.

Joseph D. Tonkin

Fascinating Facts About
Your Presidents...

The only president who served two non-consecutive terms was
   Grover Cleveland.
Two presidents received the Nobel Prize—Teddy Roosevelt and
   Woodrow Wilson.
George Washington was inaugurated in two cities.
The first president to use an automobile in his inaugural parade was
   Warren Harding.
The first president to toss in the baseball on opening day of the season
   was William Howard Taft.
John Adams lived to the most advanced age.
Eight presidents never exercised the veto.
Eleven presidents also served as vice-presidents.
Eight presidents died in office—five died without completing their
   first term.
Four presidents were assassinated—Lincoln, Garfield, McKinley,
   Kennedy.
Calvin Coolidge took the oath of office from his own father.
F.D.R. was the first president to appoint a woman to his cabinet.
Norman Thomas was nominated for the presidency six times.
James Madison was the shortest and Abe Lincoln the tallest president.
Two presidents were Federalists—George Washington and John Adams.
Two presidents' elections were decided by the House of
   Representatives—Thomas Jefferson and John Quincy Adams.
The only bachelor president was James Buchanan.
John Quincy Adams was the only president whose father was a
   president.
Benjamin Harrison was the only president whose grandfather
   was a president.
Theodore Roosevelt was the first president to go underwater in a
   submarine.
John Adams, Thomas Jefferson, James Monroe all died on the
   Fourth of July.
John Tyler had 15 children.
Ten presidents served as generals—Washington, Jackson, Taylor,
   Pierce, Grant, Hayes, Garfield, Eisenhower and both Harrisons.
Andrew Johnson was impeached and acquitted.
William Harrison gave the longest inaugural address.
J.F.K. received a Pulitzer Prize.
Five presidents served in the Continental Congresses—Washington,
   Adams, Jefferson, Madison, Monroe.

LET'S READ IT TOGETHER
THE CHILDREN'S CORNER

I Knew Christopher Columbus

My name is Lipani. I am an Indian living here in Spain. I am here because I knew Columbus.

It was I who first saw the three ships come out of the horizon like great birds. I was gathering cocoanuts on one of the highest hills in Guanahani . . . one of the Islands of the Indies.

I was not afraid when men of white skins came to our shores. I was glad. I thought they must be gods come to answer all the questions about the outside world. They had come to give me learning, and learning was what I wanted most. I was thirsty for knowledge.

One man stood out above all the rest. He carried a white banner and had a gleaming cross on the cloth which covered his chest. This man had red hair streaked with white.

When I sneaked down to the beach the big man saw me and motioned me to come to him. His smile was kind so I went to him. He tossed bright colored beads around my neck.

"I am Don Columbus," he said. Though most of the words meant nothing to me then, the kindness of his face meant a great deal. But he made me understand with his motions that he wanted me to learn to speak his language and he pointed to a man with a sword, Alfredo, indicating that this man would teach me.

Then thousands of my tribesmen came down to the shore. They chattered and grabbed at the beads, the tinkling bells, and red stocking caps. After that I went on shipboard. I studied Spanish as the three ships the Pinta, Nina and the Santa Maria sailed around the Islands. By the time we reached Cuba, Alfredo told me I was the best pupil he had ever had.

It was at this time that a bad thing happened. I heard the Captain of the Pinta say he was going to leave Don Columbus and sail his ship away. He said he would fill it with precious gold and return to Spain and claim all honors for himself.

"You do not run away from Columbus," I shouted at the man and sprang at him like I would a dangerous beast in the jungle. I knocked him down. I felt his great strength under me. I smashed my fist toward his face, but it glanced off and hit the deck with a terrible shattering shock. I was thrown off balance. Then I felt the Captain's hard hands dig into my shoulders and then I was hurled through the air! I hit the water with a stinging slap. I could not breathe.

Continued on page 86

Continued from page 85

I turned over on my back to float when I saw a spear coming at me. I dove down, down, down. But the sting in my arm told me the spear had hit. Still I knew I must swim to the Santa Maria and warn the kind man, whom I had come to love, that one ship was about to desert him.

I swam hard, though my arm pained. The hull of the Santa Maria gradually came closer. I climbed the anchor chain, as I had often climbed trees, and stumbled into the Admiral's cabin.

"The Pinta. She run away," I gasped out.

"But," said Columbus, "you are hurt! I must cleanse the wound."

"Not time!" I cried. "Go after . . . Catch . . . Ship go NOW!"

The Admiral's gentle hands had already made the pain less. He then started to light flares to signal the Pinta to come to him. I think he could not believe that the ship would desert him. Not really. Still, all night long I watched Columbus' light signals. There was no answer. By morning the Pinta was gone.

The next few days we sailed around the Cuban coast. Ship space was very valuable now since there were only two ships left. I thought maybe I would not be allowed to stay. But I wanted to stay for I loved Don Columbus and I loved learning, and now had the dream to go to Spain and study with the learned ones. One night Columbus said to me: "Be of good cheer, Lipani. This is Christmas eve." I followed the tall man to his cabin, I remember, to see

if I could be of any help to him. I did not imagine at that time that this Christmas eve would be a nightmare in my memory. Don Columbus was so tired he fell, fully clothed, on his bunk and went to sleep.

Back up on the deck I saw that the pilot had left his wheel and gone to his cabin to rest, too. A cabin boy was at the wheel. He knew almost nothing about navigation. I knew nothing of navigation either, but I knew these waters. I knew we were coming head on into a sandbar.

"Boy," I said. "You go toward sand island. You get man or you sink ship!" "Go away, you savage," he yelled back at me. "What do you know about sailing?"

It was then, as I turned to go to the cabin of the Admiral, that the ship struck. It struck softly and gently, then lodged herself forever. Columbus was first on deck. "Jump to it, men! Lower away the life boats!" I saw Columbus go back to his cabin for his precious charts and instruments and then go with the last boat to the smallest ship, the *Nina*.

The next morning Don Columbus said that all could not go back to Spain on the little Nina, there was not room. Some would have to stay in the New World and found a settlement. Thirty-nine men volunteered.

I went to Columbus then. "I can go to Spain?" I asked timidly. "I want to go where there is much learning."

He said: "I cannot refuse, Lipani. I must bring some of you people back with me to prove that I have found another route to the West Indies, and you are the most trustworthy. I cannot promise learning. That decision lies with their gracious Majesties, King Ferdinand and Queen Isabella.

Continued on page 88

Continued from page 87

After many days on the sea I became restless. I wanted to put my feet on land once more. Though the air was clear and the breeze warm I felt chills of doubt. What was going to happen to me in Spain? Don Columbus told me it was the middle of April and we would soon be ready to drop anchor in Spain.

The wonderful day came when I saw land . . . the land of my dreams! The Pinta and her Captain had not come yet. My Admiral sat high in the saddle on a fine horse. Then came seamen, the great lizards, and then six of my fellow tribesmen in their feathered headdresses, carrying javelins and bows. I was among these.

The queen called me "Delightful!" and did not stare at me peculiarly as did the people in the streets who hailed my Admiral and threw flowers before him. Don Columbus spoke to their Majesties and when he spoke of me he said: "Lipani is a fine loyal subject, Your Majesties. He is intelligent and greatly desires to acquire learning."

At that moment my heart was so full of love for the kind man that I thought everyone in Spain must be able to hear its poundings.

The Queen nodded. "He shall be tutored," she said.

I have been studying ever since. I am still seeking many answers. Here I have a chance of finding them. I am contented.

Though I have not seen my Admiral for many moons, due to a third voyage to the New World, I am waiting, and wondering if this voyage will bring him the glory and fame he deserves.

Evelyn Witter

Indian Lullaby

Rockabye, hushabye, little papoose,
The stars come into the sky.
The daylight is dying,
The whip-poor-will's crying,
The river goes murmuring by.
The pine tree is slumbering, little papoose,
The squirrel has gone to its rest.
The robins are sleeping,
The mother bird's keeping
The little ones warm with her breast.
Then hushabye, rockabye, little papoose,
You sail on the river of dreams.
Dear Manitou loves you,
And watches above you,
Till time when the morning light beams.

Author Unknown

Thanksgiving

O GIVE THANKS UNTO THE LORD, FOR HE IS GOOD:
FOR HIS MERCY ENDURETH FOREVER.

PSALMS 107:1

Little Things

Should you start to count your blessings
In the usual, off-hand way,
Much like taking inventory
As of this Thanksgiving Day,
You'll no doubt list those outstanding
With a joy that thrills and clings;
But you'll have a happier total
If you'll count the little things!

Don't forget the smiling welcome
Of the one you love so well,
Nor the peaceful evening hour
And the fireside's tranquil spell;
Don't forget the merry prattle
Of that bright-eyed, little lad,
Who perhaps loves "Mummy" mostest,
Yet is crazy 'bout his Dad!

Don't forget the pup that greets you
With a bark when work is done,
Nor a thousand homely blessings
Which are precious, everyone;
So when taking inventory,
Note the pleasure each one brings,
But be sure to make full entry—
Don't forget the little things!

Adam N. Reiter

Thanks Be To God

For life so bountiful and free,
For health that cometh, Lord, from Thee,
For strength that ever guideth me,
Thanks be to God.

For faith in Thee whate'er I do,
For hope to keep me strong and true,
For prayer that ever will subdue,
Thanks be to God.

For light that shineth day by day,
For help from Thee along the way,
For love to keep me lest I stray,
Thanks be to God.

For Christ who died on Calvary,
For Thy salvation, pure and free,
For life throughout eternity,
Thanks be to God.

Marylene Hubert

Reason To Be Grateful

We bow and praise the wonder of God's mystery on this another thanksgiving season. The trees are wearing orange and red; the yellow pumpkins are piled high on the ground and once again we feel the cool crisp air.

We are surrounded by the abundance of our lives, not for feast, but for our daily bread.

Perhaps on this day we should remember the wonderful band of people who gathered in the rough rugged earth on this cold November day over three centuries ago to give thanks for so little.

Their tables were not laden with food . . . they were happy for shelter from wind, rain and cold where they could live in freedom.

We are so grateful for this beautiful and wonderful land of ours that gives us so much to live on and the freedom that is mighty precious. May it continue long in the future.

Ann L. Bangham

Thanksgiving

This yearly festival was always kept at Plumfield in the good old-fashioned way, and nothing was allowed to interfere with it. For days beforehand, the little girls helped Asia and Mrs. Jo in storeroom and kitchen, making pies and puddings, sorting fruit, dusting dishes, and being very busy and immensely important. The boys hovered on the outskirts of the forbidden ground, sniffing the savory odors, peeping in at the mysterious performances and occasionally being permitted to taste some delicacy in the process of preparation.

When at last the day came, the boys went off for a long walk, that they might have good appetites for dinner, as if they ever needed them! The girls remained at home to help set the table and give last touches to various affairs which filled their busy little souls with anxiety.

"They are coming, I hear Emil roaring 'Land lubbers lying down below,' so we must run and dress," cried Nan, and upstairs they scampered in a great hurry.

The boys came trooping home with appetites that would have made the big turkey tremble, if it had not been past all fear. They also retired to dress; and for half an hour there was a washing, brushing, and prinking that would have done any tidy woman's heart good to see. When the bell rang, a troop of fresh-faced lads with shiny hair, clean collars, and Sunday jackets on, filed into the dining room, where Mrs. Jo, in her one black silk, with a knot of her favorite white chrysanthemums in her bosom, sat at the head of the table, "looking splendid," as the boys said, whenever she got herself up. Daisy and Nan were as gay as a posy bed in their new winter dresses, with bright sashes and hair ribbons. Teddy was gorgeous to behold in a crimson merino blouse and his best button boots, which absorbed and distracted him as much as Mr. Toot's wristbands did on one occasion.

As Mr. and Mrs. Bhaer glanced at each other down the long table, with those rows of happy faces on either side, they had a little thanksgiving, all to themselves, and without a word, for one heart said to the other, "Our work has prospered, let us be grateful and go on."

The clatter of knives and forks prevented much conversation for a few minutes, and Mary Ann with an amazing pink bow in her hair "flew around" briskly, handing plates and ladling out gravy. Nearly every one had contributed to the feast, so the dinner was a peculiarly interesting one to the eaters of it, who beguiled the pauses by remarks on their own productions.

"If these are not good potatoes I never saw any," observed Jack, as he received his fourth big mealy one.

Continued on page 94

Continued from page 93

"Some of my herbs are in the stuffing of the turkey, that's why it's so nice," said Nan, taking a mouthful with intense satisfaction.

"My ducks are prime anyway, Asia said she never cooked such fat ones," added Tommy.

"Well, our carrots are beautiful, ain't they, and our parsnips will be ever so good when we dig them," put in Dick, and Dolly murmured his assent from behind the bone he was picking.

"I helped make the pies with my pumpkin," called out Robby, with a laugh which he stopped by retiring into his mug.

"I picked some of the apples that the cider is made of," said Demi.

"I raked the cranberries for the sauce," cried Nat.

"I got the nuts," added Dan, and so it went on all round the table.

"Who made up Thanksgiving?" asked Rob, for being lately promoted to jacket and trousers he felt a new and manly interest in the institutions of his country.

"See who can answer that question," and Mr. Bhaer nodded to one or two of his best history boys.

"I know," said Demi, "the Pilgrims made it."

"What for?" asked Rob, without waiting to learn who the Pilgrims were.

"I forget," and Demi subsided.

"I believe it was because they were not starved once, and so when they had a good harvest, they said, 'We will thank God for it,' and they had a day and called it Thanksgiving," said Dan, who liked the story of the brave men who suffered so nobly for their faith.

"Good! I didn't think you would remember any thing but natural history," and Mr. Bhaer, tapped gently on the table as applause for his pupil.

Dan looked pleased, and Mrs. Jo said to her son, "Now do you understand about it, Robby?"

"No, I don't. I thought pil-grins were a sort of big bird that lived on rocks, and I saw pictures of them in Demi's book."

"He means penguins. Oh, isn't he a little goosey!" and Demi laid back in his chair and laughed aloud.

"Don't laugh at him, but tell him all about it if you can," said Mrs. Bhaer, consoling Rob with more cranberry sauce for the general smile that went round the table at his mistake.

"Well, I will," and, after a pause to collect his ideas, Demi delivered the following sketch of the Pilgrim Fathers, which would have made even those grave gentlemen smile if they could have heard it.

"You see, Rob, some of the people in England didn't like the king, or something, so they got into ships and sailed away to this country. It was all full of Indians, and bears, and wild creatures, and they lived in forts and had a dreadful time."

"The bears?" asked Robby, with interest.

"No, the Pilgrims, because the Indians troubled them. They hadn't enough to eat, and they went to church with guns, and ever so many died, and they got out of the ships on a rock, and it's called Plymouth Rock, and Aunt Jo saw it and touched it. The Pilgrims killed all the Indians and got rich, and hung the witches, and were very good, and some of my greatest great-grandpas came in the ships. One was the Mayflower, and they made Thanksgiving, and we have it always, and I like it. Some more turkey, please."

"I think Demi will be an historian, there is such order and clearness in his account of events," and Uncle Fritz's eyes laughed at Aunt Jo, as he helped the descendant of the Pilgrims to his third bit of turkey.

"I thought you must eat as much as ever you could on Thanksgiving. But Franz says you mustn't even then," and Stuffy looked as if he had received bad news.

"Franz is right, so mind your knife and fork, and be moderate, or else you won't be able to help in the surprise by and by," said Mrs. Jo.

"I'll be careful, but everybody does eat lots, and I like it better than being moderate," said Stuffy, who leaned to the popular belief that Thanksgiving must be kept by coming as near apoplexy as possible and escaping with merely a fit of indigestion or a headache.

"Now, my 'pilgrims' amuse yourselves quietly till tea time, for you will have enough excitement this evening," said Mrs. Jo, as they rose from the table after a protracted sitting, finished by drinking every one's health in cider.

"I think I will take the whole flock for a drive, it is so pleasant, then you can rest, my dear, or you will be worn out this evening," added Mr. Bhaer, and as soon as coats and hats could be put on, the great omnibus was packed full, and away they went for a long gay drive, leaving Mrs. Jo to rest and finish sundry small affairs in peace.

Louisa May Alcott

GOLdEN VERSE

Falling Leaves?

They are silent?—oh!
Each falling leaf is like a
thump upon my heart!

Eleanor DiGiulio

Harvest

What do I hold
Of harvest from the past?
The orange moon at Hallowe'en
As children's feet scuffed through dried leaves;
An orchard view of apples everywhere
On bending boughs, red, yellow, streaked,
A mellow afternoon of ripened fruit;
Thanksgiving dinner served by a great-grandmother
Who made nine decades seem a natural thing.
What do I hold of harvest now
To add to all the hours of purple haze
That I have kept in memory?
I add this day of maple flame and air
That brings the mountains nearer to the sea,
Vivid statement of autumn splendor.

Louise Darcy

Thank You, Lord

Thank you, Lord.
—for loving us even when we have despised you;
—for seeking us even when we have not looked for you;
—for guiding us perhaps most carefully and precisely when we think
we are quite able of finding our own way;
—for giving us tasks that we neither want nor can do;
—for giving us critics and those who disagree with us when we would
rather have approval and agreement;
—for seeing us as children when we see ourselves as managers of the
universe;
—for being present with men even when they deny your existence;
—for giving blessings like this that remind us we are men—and not
gods.

Adele Anderson

Spring Will Come

Like ghostly passing phantoms
The leaves fall, one by one
Rime lays across the landscape
A thick haze veils the sun

Corn shocks stand in the meadows
Like sentinels, stately, grand
With pumpkins, golden yellow
Gifts from God's bounteous hand

'Cross mountain, fen, and woodland
O'er all, a silence deep
Dame nature's getting ready
To take her winter's sleep

But do not grieve her resting,
Ye mortal sons of men
For soon will end her beauty nap
And she'll awake again

The brooks will start to murmur
The birds awake to song
The trees put on new dress of green
The days again grow long

The voice of sowing farmer
Be heard across the dell
God smiles, the meadows come abloom
Again, and all is well.

George E. Blanchard

GOLDEN PRAYER

Give thanks unto him for a remembrance
   of his holiness.
For his wrath endureth but the twinkling
   of an eye, and in his pleasure in life:
Heaviness may endure for a night but joy
   cometh in the morning.

The Book of Common Prayer

October Caught Me Dreaming

Drowned in the hot sweet silence on the hill,
Fragrant with apples and warm summer hay,
I watched the shadows shimmer and grow still
As evening drew dim curtains on the day.

Each thunder-haunted night and purple noon
Flowed through my soul into eternity;
Summer, adorned with jeweled hours of June,
Matured into October tapestry.

I had not heard the faded petals fall,
Felt thistledown float past me in the air;
I had not wakened to shrill cricket-call,
October caught me dreaming, unaware.

Her faint blue wood-smoke spiraled up the sky,
The shadow of my heart's unanswered cry.

Alice Mackenzie Swaim

An Early Morning Walk

Thank You, Lord, for early morning,
When the first golden fingers
Of sunshine
Slant sharply upward,
Touching only the tops of the tallest trees,
Then move gently downward,
Warming houses and yards
In yellow light.
Before the busy-ness begins,
Thank You, Lord,
For a new, quiet, untouched day.

Annice Harris Brown

Thanksgiving Day

There's something that is cheery-like around Thanksgiving time,
That makes a person feel as though the season's in its prime;
There's something in the atmosphere that seems to hold a charm,
That takes the city folks way back to childhood and the farm.
I can't explain just what it is, but it is not a dream,
These pictures and their colorings, no painter's pen can gleam;
For nature has provided well, rich bounties to adorn
The homestead, when the family meets upon Thanksgiving morn.

And while the season's barren, with some snowflakes in the air,
Somehow all worry's vanished and we're free from every care;
A sense of rarest gratitude is spreading through the room,
Erasing every atom of lament and doubt and gloom.
There's ecstasy abundant through November's chilly days,
And air is appetizing at the time of sleds and sleighs.
The purple fields have yielded all their shocks of ripened corn
And the world is rich with many blessings on Thanksgiving morn.

We miss the turkey's gobble, as he used to strut around,
And all the golden pumpkins that were lying on the ground;
But now the oven's lighted and its odors seem to rise
Of turkey and its dressing, and of good old pumpkin pies.
There's fruit cake and plum pudding with a tasty sauce atop,
And candied sweet potatoes—well, I simply have to stop.
It's useless that I try to tell of joys that take full sway,
When the family gets together on a glad Thanksgiving day.

Tessa Sweazy Webb

The Governor's Son

More than anything young John Bradford wanted to be alone. Barefoot, he climbed up the rope ladder of the mainmast to the crosstrees, fifty-four feet above the deck. Filled with a deep longing he clung to the swaying mast.

Over two months had gone by this year of 1627 since the ship had sailed for Plymouth, Massachusetts, from Leyden, Holland, a place he had learned to call home.

He remembered well that day seven years ago when he was only five years old, his father saying, "It's not easy to let go of somebody you love." Then his parents sailed with the other Pilgrims aboard the *Mayflower* to the New World.

He had been left in the care of Pastor John Robinson. The land and the ways of the Dutch people were strange, but he had learned the new language quickly. He joined the Dutch boys and girls skating on the frozen canals in winter, fishing in summer, and exploring fascinating windmills. He had eaten good and plentiful Dutch food and grown lean with strong muscles.

John's eye swept the horizon. The wind was still blowing from last night's storm but the skies were clear.

What had made his father send for him after seven long years? Was it because he had remarried after John's mother had died, or was it because Pastor John Robinson had passed away two years ago?

John did not know. He felt he belonged to no one. Then he grinned wryly, thinking of the time when he was ten and he had stowed away on a ship bound for the New World, only to be caught and sent back to Holland. Every year the wish to see the New World grew stronger until suddenly it seemed to fill his whole body.

Then the letter had arrived. His father had sent for him—his father wanted him—his father needed him. No longer would he feel alone.

John clung tightly to the swaying mast. The weather was different here on the ocean. Overnight the weather could change. Savage storms would come sweeping out of the west. The salty sea water constantly pounded the main deck.

Yesterday, a huge wave had suddenly swept over the deck and tossed John into the sea! Just as he went over the stern his hand grabbed one of the ropes used to hoist sails. Frantically he had clung to the rope, burning blisters on his hands. Faintly he thought he had heard someone call to hold on. A boathook was thrust within his reach. A strong seaman had heaved and pulled John scrambling and gasping for breath back on board ship. He was taken below, shivering and sick, but a good night's sleep had speeded his recovery.

Impatiently John scanned the horizon again. He saw a peculiar cloud formation. He looked away for a few seconds, then looked back. The formation remained unchanged. It was not a cloud!

"Land ho! Land ho!" he shouted.

Instantly everyone rushed on deck. "Aye, I agree with you, lad," called the captain from below.

It was not long after that the anchor chain rumbled as the huge hook dropped to the ocean's floor in the harbor.

Once ashore, John sprinted ahead. It felt good to stretch one's legs in a long run up and down the sand!

Suddenly he collided with a heavy-set man who grabbed him by the shoulders. The bearded man's face was beaming.

"John! Welcome home!"

John felt himself spun around to face the man and a woman with small children clinging shyly to her skirts. He was introduced to his new mother and stepbrothers and stepsisters.

Home! John thought the word had music in it.

"Race you!" he called to the children. Eagerly they sped after him. Then he slowed his pace to theirs, seeing not canals, windmills, or tulips as in Holland, but rather a line of thatched huts along two streets leading straight up a hill to a fort enclosed in a high palisade.

He looked back over his shoulder proudly at his father, the Governor, who had written that he *needed* his son to be with him as one of the family. John knew that was what *he* wanted more than anything else—to be needed as one of a family again.

Phyllis M. Hemphill

Thanksgiving Day

This is the time, that special time,
The day we set apart
To try to voice the gratitude
We feel deep in our heart.

The time when we become aware
Of blessings, great and small,
And realize we never can
Give proper thanks to all.

But since God understands and hears
The language of the heart,
I'm sure He knows and cherishes
This day we set apart.

Helen Lowrie Marshall

Autumn Splendor

The golds, and reds, the gorgeous browns
The beauties everywhere,
The big orange pumpkins in the corn
The scent of autumn air,
The rustle of the falling leaves
The harvest moon above,
And all the million other signs
That bring the time we love.

The autumn stream slows up a bit
And autumn nights are cool,
And youngsters with their books and slates
Are going back to school,
September is a precious month
With summer days just through,
And such a very pleasant time
For all we plan to do.

The autumn brings us harvest time
The orchard all aglow,
A flame of red against the sky
That seems to sparkle so,
The old rail fence is lovely now
With goldenrod in bloom,
A melancholy autumn breeze
Puts all the world in tune.

Tis autumn on the woodland path
And on the hill afar,
The autumn shines in valleys gold
And lights an autumn star,
The grandest time of all the year
It's Mother Nature's show,
When Autumn Splendor crowns the world
And sets our hearts aglow.

Garnett Ann Schultz

Let's Read It Together
the children's corner

Talking Turkey

Charles Sawyer was a Pilgrim lad
Who, feeling very perky
One misty day, set out to hunt
The wild New England turkey.
He scurried through the brush and bog
And hid himself behind a log;
And there he made a scratchy-squawk
That sounded much like turkey talk. . . .

An Indian, with colored feather,
That very morning wondered whether
He, too, could catch some gobbler game
And through the selfsame woods he came.
On hands and knees, instead of walking,
He crept, and also made a squawking
Till he and Charlie—calling, talking
Back and forth with gibberish word—
Each thought the other was a bird;

And, as they sought each other's place
Of hiding, they came face to face.
Then shots that might have followed after
Were changed to sudden peals of laughter.

The Indian, though just a grunter,
Told Charlie he was quite a hunter;
And Charlie, signing with his hand,
Soon made the red man understand
He much admired his decoying.
So off they went, those two, enjoying

Their little joke; and when a jerky
Wattled head peered through the murky
Morning at them, each cried "Turkey!"

Continued on page 104

Continued from page 103

The quiet bowshot and the louder
Gunshot with its smell of powder
Brought the bird down in a minute
An arrow and a bullet in it.

Then such a feast the hunters had
Beside the fire! Lad and lad
Forgetting they were enemies
Among the wood anemones.
The fun led to friendly living
And to the Pilgrims' first
THANKSGIVING.

Rowena Bennett

Happy Thanksgiving!

Soon Thanksgiving Day will come. People will say "Happy Thanksgiving!" to each other. We will say "Thank you" to God for our food and home and family and friends. We will be thankful for sunshine and rain and everything that makes the world beautiful. And we'll laugh and sing and have a good thanksgiving dinner and a happy time.

Many children will play they are Pilgrim girls and boys who came here long ago and enjoyed their Thanksgiving Day in America. They had sailed across the ocean with their mothers and fathers on a little ship called the "Mayflower." The Pilgrims had left their homes in England because in those days they were not allowed to pray together and worship God in the way they thought was right.

As the "Mayflower" sailed toward America, cold winds whistled through its sails. The Pilgrims kept wondering about this new country where they would live. In that long-ago time there were no cities in America. There were very few people in the big woods or along the seashore.

The Pilgrims knew that Indians lived here. And sometimes the Indians were friendly to people from across the ocean. Often they fought the new people. The Pilgrims were going far from their old homes, but they made up their minds to be brave and work hard. They were determined to make pleasant homes in the new country for their families.

After many weeks at sea someone on the "Mayflower" shouted "Land, ho!" Every one rushed on deck to look. How glad they were to see land after such a long trip on the crowded ship!

Before they went ashore, the Pilgrim leaders talked with everybody. If they wanted to build homes and make little gardens and farms and start a good little town, they must all help each other. So, the men signed a paper promising they would work together for the best good of everyone. And they would obey the laws that were made.

Later some men went to shore in a small boat, to get wood and see what the land was like. They brought back armfuls of sweet-smelling pinewood and some sprigs of red holly berries for the children.

Soon the women and children went to shore, bobbing through the water in the small boat. They took great bundles of clothes to be washed. The children ran along the seashore and laughed and shouted and sang. They helped gather wood for fires to heat the wash water. They looked for nut trees. They skipped stones out into the bay. They helped spread the wash to dry on fragrant-smelling sassafras bushes and low junipers. They took pine cones and walnuts back to the "Mayflower" with them.

Many days passed, though, before they all left the "Mayflower" to live on land. First the men had to find just the right place to build their homes. They chose a place called Plymouth, on high ground near the shore, with a little brook and springs of water. There they would start the Pilgrim's Plymouth Colony.

Even though winter had begun, the men began to build houses in Plymouth. Their axes sounded "thud, thud" through the woods as they chopped down trees. Soon their hammers pounded as they built some houses.

That winter was very hard for everyone, both those on shore and on the "Mayflower." Many people were very sick. They tried to nurse each other. They were all cold and hungry. Sometimes Indians shot arrows when the Pilgrim men were in the woods. Wolves howled around them. Wild winds blew down part of the houses before they were finished. But the men kept on working, building houses to shelter everyone. And people crowded together in the first houses.

At last springtime was near. Birds began to sing in the woods. Suddenly, one sunny day an Indian came to Plymouth. All alone! The pilgrim children ran to their homes to tell their mothers. Then they peeped from doorways as the Indian walked to the place where the Pilgrim leaders were talking.

The children hurried closer to look and listen. Everyone was surprised when the Indian spoke English as they did. His name was Samoset. He had learned English from fishermen who came to fish at

Continued on page 106

Continued from page 105

an Island farther up the seacoast. He told them about different Indian tribes; and the Pilgrims gave him roast duck, biscuits, and butter and pudding to eat.

Later, Samoset brought another Indian, named Squanto. The Pilgrims were pleased that Squanto showed them how to plant corn and helped them in many ways. Samoset and Squanto brought the Indian chief Massasoit to meet the Pilgrims. He was a good friend to them. He and they agreed always to be friends and to help each other.

Pilgrim girls and boys worked hard helping plant corn the way Squanto showed them. All summer the Pilgrims worked together fixing their new homes and taking care of their little farms. They wanted to grow enough so they would have extra food to store for next winter.

When leaves on the trees began turning yellow and red, the Pilgrims' little gardens and farms were ready to harvest. They said, "Let's have a harvest feast and thank God for all we have. Let's invite Massasoit and some of his Indians to share the good time."

Everybody in Plymouth got busy for the thanksgiving feast. Some men went into the woods and brought back wild turkeys and geese and other meat. Men and boys went fishing. The children dug clams and picked wild grapes and beach plums. They all helped gather the corn and other vegetables. The women and big girls began cooking the good things to eat.

At last the day of thanksgiving came. Savory smells of roasting meat and of corn and of cakes filled the air. Out of the woods came Chief Massasoit with ninety Indians! They listened quietly while the Pilgrims thanked God for giving them such a good harvest and for taking care of them in this new land.

Then they all gathered around and ate and ate. They laughed and joked together and ate some more. Then the Indians and the Pilgrims ran races and saw how far they could shoot arrows and jumped and wrestled.

Chief Massasoit sent some Indians hunting, and they brought back more meat to roast. So the thanksgiving feast lasted three days. Perhaps during that time some Indians showed the Pilgrim children how to pop corn and gave them corn to pop. Perhaps the Indians sang some of their harvest songs for the Pilgrims, and the Pilgrims sang their songs for the Indians.

That was a Thanksgiving Day the Pilgrims never forgot. In time, all over our great big country people heard the story of the Pilgrims' thanksgiving. And for many years Thanksgiving has been a happy holiday throughout our whole United States of America. Happy Thanksgiving to everybody!

Mildred Corell Luckhardt

Friendship

To A Friend

You entered my life in a casual way,
  And saw at a glance what I needed;
There were others who passed me or met me each day,
  But never a one of them heeded.
Perhaps you were thinking of other folks more,
  Or chance simply seemed to decree it;
I know there were many such chances before,
  But the others—well, they didn't see it.

You said just the thing that I wished you would say,
And you made me believe that you meant it;
I held up my head in the old gallant way,
  And resolved you should never repent it.
There are times when encouragement means such a lot,
  And a word is enough to convey it;
There were others who could have, as easy as not—
  But, just the same, they didn't say it.

There may have been someone who could have done more
  To help me along, though I doubt it;
What I needed was cheering, and always before
  They had let me plod onward without it.
You have helped to refashion the dream of my heart,
  And made me turn eagerly to it;
There were others who might have (I question that part)—
  But, after all, they didn't do it!

Grace Stricker Dawson

You Get What You Give

You get what you give
In like and in kind,
The trust you instill
Is that which you find.
The joy that you spread,
Must ever return,
A lamp must be filled
Before it will burn.

You get what you give
In gladness or woe,
A seed must be planted
Before it will grow.
There must be a dream
For it to come true,
And he who would dare,
Must learn how to do.

You get what you give,
Don't ever expect
Life to give more
Than she can collect.
All things are weighed
On the scales up above,
And he is found wanting,
. . . Who's empty of love.

Grace E. Easley

GOLDEN THOUGHT

He gives little who gives with a frown; he gives
much who gives a little with a smile.

The Talmud

Bond Of Friendship

A true friend to me, is as the pearl to the oyster—
Two separate beings joined as one.
The oyster shell when opened, and the pearl plucked
    from its bed,
Is the bond of friendship . . . broken.

Gloria L. Vaughan

Your Neighbor

Do you know the neighbor who lives in your block;
Do you even take time for a bit of talk?
Do you know his troubles, his heartaches, his cares,
The battles he's fighting, the burdens he bears?
Do you greet him with joy or pass him right by
With a questioning look and a quizzical eye?
Do you bid him "Good morning" and "How do you do,"
Or shrug up as if he was nothing to you?
He may be a chap with a mighty big heart,
And a welcome that grips, if you just do your part.
And I know you'll coax out his sunniest smile,
If you'll stop with this neighbor and visit awhile.

We rush on so fast in these strenuous days,
We're apt to find fault when it's better to praise.
We judge a man's worth by the make of his car;
We're anxious to find what his politics are.
But somehow it seldom gets under the hide,
The fact that the fellow we're living beside
Is a fellow like us, with a hankering, too,
For a grip of the hand and a "How do you do!"

With a heart that responds in a welcome sincere
If you'll just stop to fling him a message of cheer,
And I know you'll coax out his sunniest smile,
If you'll stop with this neighbor and visit awhile.

H. Howard Biggar

Zacchaeus Finds a Friend

In the whole city of Jericho there was no man more hated than Zacchaeus the rich tax collector. In the first place people hated him because he worked for the Romans, their enemies, in collecting taxes from them. The Romans demanded that Zacchaeus turn over to them a certain amount of tax money, but they paid their tax collectors no wages. Instead, they charged these men for the privilege of collecting taxes. Each of them was free to collect as much money from the people as he could force them to pay. What remained after the Roman government got their share, the tax collector could keep for himself. As you can imagine, most tax collectors were greedy men; they actually forced the people to pay outrageously. The more the collectors took from the people, the more they were hated. And the more they were hated, the more they made the people pay.

So, though Zacchaeus lived in a fine house and had everything that money could buy, he was a very lonely man. No neighbors knocked at his door and came in to visit with him. No one ever greeted him or spoke a friendly word when he passed along the street. Zacchaeus would gladly have parted with much of his money just to hear some man call him friend, but not all his gold and silver could buy him that pleasure.

One day Zacchaeus sat at the table where his townsmen came to pay their taxes. Carefully he checked each man's name in a book as the man turned over his money. Zacchaeus tried to pretend he did not hear the angry mutterings of the men as he took their money and passed over their receipts. If any man looked as though he would refuse to pay or wanted to start a fight, a Roman soldier was always standing close to the taxpayer's elbow. All Zacchaeus had to do was to glance at the angry man and nod to the waiting soldier. Then, presto! The rebellious taxpayer would find himself on the way to prison.

In the midst of Zacchaeus' work there was a commotion in the crowd. A man ran up and called out breathlessly, "Jesus is coming! He is only a little way behind me."

At once the crowd stirred and turned to the road where Jesus must pass. Everyone had heard of the wonderful things Jesus was saying and doing. All of them wanted to see Jesus. Zacchaeus wanted to see him too, but he was a little man and not very strong. He could not see over the heads of the crowd. Try as he would, he could not force his way through the crowd. Perhaps the people were blocking him because they hated him so.

But Zacchaeus was a clever little man. "All right!" he told himself. "I'll see Jesus even if I have to climb a tree to do it." And that is just what he did! Nimbly he scrambled up a great sycamore tree that stood nearby and hid himself among the branches. From his high perch he could see better than anyone. Shading his eyes from the sun's glare, he peered down eagerly as he saw Jesus approaching.

"What a friendly smiling face Jesus has!" thought Zacchaeus longingly. "It must be wonderful to have a friend like that." Imagine his astonishment then to see Jesus stop right under his tree. He could not believe his ears when Jesus called out to him.

"Zacchaeus!"

But Zacchaeus was too surprised to make a sound. "How does he know my name?" he wondered, greatly puzzled. "And how was he able to see me hidden among the tree branches?"

"Zacchaeus!" Again that warm and friendly voice called his name. "Zacchaeus, come down. I must stay at your house today."

Never did Zacchaeus move faster than he did then. In an instant he threw his arms around the trunk of the tree, slid down to the ground, and stood facing Jesus.

"Did you say, Jesus," Zacchaeus asked timidly, "that you would stay at my house? Do—do you know what I am?"

"He is a sinner!" one of the Pharisees standing by exclaimed spitefully. "There is no man so despised in all Jericho."

Zacchaeus bowed his head in shame. Every word was true. He was indeed a sinful man, a cheat, taking every penny he could get from his neighbors. But he hoped that this kind teacher would be his friend anyhow. "I would not be so wicked," he whispered, scarcely daring to look up from the dusty road, "if I had even one friend."

"I have come to be your friend, Zacchaeus," Jesus said gently, as he put his hand on Zacchaeus' bowed shoulder. "Come, I am hungry and need a place to rest. Will you not invite me to your home?"

"Oh, please come with me," answered Zacchaeus joyfully. "My wife will make a fine supper for you, and you shall rest your tired body on my couch."

The Pharisees heard Zacchaeus' words. They saw Jesus walking with his arm about Zacchaeus' shoulders. They listened as Jesus and the hated tax collector talked together in low tones. "Look!" they pointed scornfully, "He is going to visit the worst sinner in town!"

"Lord," the people heard Zacchaeus say, and they could see the bright tears in his eyes as he looked up into the face of Jesus, "I have indeed done wrong. I have returned hate for hate. I have charged the townspeople more than I should. I am ashamed." And Zacchaeus bowed his head and wept for all the selfish, greedy things that he had done.

"Be comforted, Zacchaeus," Jesus smiled down at the bowed head. "I came to be a friend to just such men as you, men who mean to do

Continued on page 114

Continued from page 113

better. I came to seek out and to save those who know what it is to feel lost and lonely."

"I will never cheat again," Zacchaeus promised, knowing that he had been forgiven by his new friend. "Those whom I have cheated, I will give back to them four times as much as I took from them wrongfully." He looked up again at the loving face of Jesus turned toward him. "I will do more," he added eagerly. "I will give half of all I have left to the poor. As I have found a friend in you, Master, I will be a friend to them."

That was a day that Zacchaeus never forgot. He had indeed found what money cannot buy, a true and loving friend.

Elizabeth Whitehouse

Contentment

If I can lend a helping hand
To you, my friend, and understand
Your need, and give to you
A surety of friendship true,
    I'll be content.

If I can share with you a grief,
And help you see at most it's brief;
If I can hold your hand in mine
Through moments of a testing time,
    I'll be content.

If I can coax your weary eyes
To look above, to fairer skies;
If I can cause your ears to hear
The music of the heavenly sphere,
    I'll be content.

If I can guide you to the place
Of prayer, where by His watchless grace
Your soul will be restored and blessed,
Where God can do for you the rest—
    I'll be content.

Roselyn C. Steere

Barriers Broken

The van comes to move you far away
Tears well in my eyes at the thought;
Still you talk to God in my behalf
And I intercede for you.
So, we are very near.

Your form of worship to me is strange
Mine, quite as strange to you;
But you love Jesus, trust in Him
Who is my Savior, too.
So, we are very near.

Young, strong, anxious to change your world
(Tho' I move cautiously)—
You are committed to follow Him
Whom I trusted years ago.
So, we are very near.

In God's varied scheme of things:
You one color, I another,
Customs, habits, clothing differ,
Yet, we love and serve one Master.
Yes, we are very near!

Leota Campbell

GOLDEN NUGGET

Anyone who out of goodness of his heart speaks a helpful word, gives a cheering smile, or smooths over a rough place in another's path knows that the delight he feels is so intimate a part of himself that he lives by it.

Helen Keller

GOLDEN THOUGHT

Friendship is the only cement that will ever hold the world together.

Woodrow Wilson

What to Forget

Forget each kindness that you do
    As soon as you have done it,
Forget the praise that falls to you
    The moment you have won it,
Forget the slanders that you hear
    Before you can repeat it,
Forget each slight, each spite, each sneer,
    Wherever you may meet it.

Remember every kindness done
    To you what e'er its measure,
Remember praise by others won
    And pass it on with pleasure,
Remember every promise made
    And keep it to the letter,
Remember those who lend you aid,
    And be a grateful debtor.

Remember all the happiness
    That comes your way in living;
Forget each worry and distress,
    Be hopeful and forgiving,
Remember good, remember truth
    Remember heaven's above you
And you will find through age and youth
    True joys, and hearts to love you.

Priscilla Leonard

Love, For The Moments are Fleeting

Love, for the moments are fleeting,
Love, for the days pass from view,
Love, for in sharing with others,
Affection is mirrored to you.

Sow gentle seeds in mild April,
And water them kindly in May.
Tend them with care in the summer,
For reaping is not far away.

For by the sweet golden of autumn
The seeds we have planted with care
Have grown into fruit of the harvest
To bless us with love and a prayer.

Viola J. Berg

gOldEN VERSE

If we give love and sympathy
Even to those who hate us
We fill them so with mystery
They know not how to rate us.

Helen King

Confide In A Friend

When you're tired and worn at the close of day
And things just don't seem to be going your way,
When even your patience has come to an end,
Try taking time out and confide in a friend.

Author Unknown

Leave A Touch Of Glory

Have you watched the sun descending
In a cloud-filled, stormy sky—
How it leaves a golden halo
As it bids the day goodby?

Here a touch of glory lingers
Like a blessing on the land—
A touch of golden glory
From a strong and unseen Hand.

There are those whose lives remind us
Of the sunset's warming glow.—
They leave a touch of glory
Lingering after when they go.

Author Unknown

golden scripture

Love is patient and kind;
love is not jealous or boastful;
it is not arrogant or rude.
Love does not insist on its own way;
it is not irritable or resentful;
it does not rejoice at wrong,
but rejoices in the right.
    Love
        bears all things,
        believes all things,
        hopes all things,
        endures all things.
Love never ends . . .

I Corinthians 13:4-8

Friendship

A friend is a source of celebration when you feel there is nothing to celebrate.

A friend is simply one who answers when you call . . . who often answers before you call.

A friend is one who is not hard to find when you are penniless.

A friend is one who makes your grief less painful, your adversity more bearable.

A friend is one who makes your disappointment less hurtful, your problem more solvable.

A friend is one who joyfully sings with you when you are on the mountain top, and silently walks beside you through the valley.

       ❖   ❖   ❖

A friend is one with whom you are comfortable, to whom you are loyal, through whom you are blessed, and for whom you are grateful.

A friend is one who warms you by his presence, trusts you with his secrets, and remembers you in his prayers.

A friend is one who gives you the spark of assurance when you doubt your ability to fulfill your destiny, to climb your mountain.

A true friend is an earthly treasure whom God lends you to help prepare your eyes, heart, mind and soul for the glories He has prepared for you.

William Arthur Ward

golden Nugget

Love all God's creation, the whole and every grain of sand in it. Love every leaf, every ray of God's light. Love the animals, love the plants, love everything. If you love everything, you will perceive the divine mystery in things. Once you perceive it, you will begin to comprehend it better every day. And you will come at last to love the whole world with an all-embracing love.

Fyodor Dostoyevsky

New Friend

There's a special little halo
That crowns the days that end
With the happy, warming knowledge
That you've made a brand-new friend.

Though you wouldn't take a fortune
For the old friends that are yours,
The making of a new friend
Always opens other doors.

Your world is wider, richer
With every new friend won,
With the hope of glad tomorrows
In a friendship just begun.

A special little halo
Gives that day a brighter hue,
And a very special halo
Crowns the day that I found you!

Author Unknown

A Shaft of Sunlight

A shaft of sunlight breaking through
Can make the whole world shining new;
Can shape tomorrow, change a life;
Can banish doubt and fear and strife.

One shaft of sunlight through the grey—
One word of cheer that we may say,
Could carry farflung consequence,
And might make all the difference.

Helen Lowrie Marshall

The Precious Friend

I have a Friend so precious,
   So very dear to me!
He loves me with such tender love,
   He loves so faithfully,
I could not live apart from Him,
   I love to feel Him nigh;
And so we dwell together,
   My Lord and I.

Sometimes I'm faint and weary;
   He knows that I am weak,
And as He bids me lean on Him,
   His help I gladly seek;
He leads me in the paths of light,
   Beneath a sunny sky;
And so we walk together,
   My Lord and I.

He knows how much I love Him.
   He knows I love Him well;
But with what love He loveth me,
   My tongue can never tell;
It is an everlasting love,
   An ever rich supply;
And so we love each other,
   My Lord and I.

Author Unknown

Let's Read It Together

the children's corner

Fire

Doug could see the smoke rising. He knew it must be at Tim's ranch. He knew, too, that Tim had been angry at him since the day Doug was chosen captain of the baseball team.

"I don't have time to go home to tell my father," he said to himself. Then Doug knew that he must hurry to Tim's ranch.

"Go like the wind," said Doug. White Star ran as fast as he could go.

They came nearer and nearer to the ranch. Then Doug could see that it was the barn burning. White Star jumped over the fence. "To the house, White Star," said Doug. White Star ran to the house. Doug jumped off. He ran to the door. He knocked but no one came.

"I must call the fire department," Doug said. He put his hand on the door. It was open. He ran inside to the telephone. He called the fire department. "We will be there as fast as we can," said the fireman. "Are there any animals in the barn?"

"I don't know," said Doug. "I'll look."

Doug ran to the barn. White Star ran, too. Doug saw smoke. But he could not see any flames. "The hay must be on fire," he said. "But what if some animals are in there?"

Doug took the rope from his saddlebag. He tied one end to White Star. He took the rest of the rope with him. Then he crawled under the smoke into the barn.

Doug crawled into the horse stalls. But the horses were not there. Doug started to crawl back. Then he felt something on the floor.

"Tim!" shouted Doug. But Tim did not answer.

Doug tied the end of the rope he was carrying to Tim's ankles. "Walk, White Star, walk," he called. White Star pulled. Doug crawled with Tim, holding onto him so he could find his way out.

Soon Doug and Tim were out of the barn. Doug saw the fire trucks coming. One fireman put something over Tim's nose and mouth.

"This will help him breathe," he said. The other firemen ran into the barn with hoses from the big fire truck.

Then they came out again. "You called us just in time," they said. "Some of the hay had caught fire. It wasn't burning fast. So it didn't burn any of the barn."

The firemen and Doug watched Tim. Soon his eyes began to open. "The barn," he said. "The barn's on fire."

The firemen smiled. "Not now," they said. "We put the fire out. But what were you doing in the barn?"

"I went in to let the horses and cows out," said Tim. "I got them all out. But the smoke got so thick I couldn't find my way out."

"It's a good thing your friend saw the smoke," said one fireman. "And it's a good thing he called us," said another fireman. "And it's a good thing he went in to find you," said a third fireman.

"And it's a good thing Doug is a better friend to me than I have been to him," said Tim.

Doug was glad. But all he said was, "It's a good thing White Star was here. I couldn't have done any of it if he hadn't helped me."

David C. Cook

Poor Little Rich King

Once, in a land far, far away there lived a king. He lived in a big castle. He had many rich things in the castle. He had tall thrones and big tables. He had big rooms and long bridges going into the castle. Some people said that the king had everything.

Well, that was the trouble. The king had *almost* everything. But he didn't have quite everything.

Whenever the king saw the knight ride his beautiful horse past the castle, he felt sad and lonely. "I want that horse so I can ride like the knight," said the king.

Whenever the king saw the village boy go past the castle with his dog, he felt sad and lonely. The boy had trained the dog to do many wonderful tricks. "I want that dog so I can have him do many tricks for me," said the king.

Whenever the king saw the minstrel, or harp player, go past the castle, he felt sad and lonely. "If I had his harp," said the king, "then I could play beautiful music, too."

Each day the king grew sadder. If only he had these things, then he would have everything. Then he would not be sad and lonely.

But the knight, the boy, and the minstrel never stopped at the castle. They knew that the king did not want to be friends with them. All he wanted were their things.

One day the king pounded his fist on his biggest table. "This is silly," he said. "I am the king. I can have anything I want."

So the king called some soldiers to him. "Bring me the knight's horse," he said.

Continued on page 124

Continued from page 123

He called some more soldiers. "Bring me the boy's dog," he said.

Then he called more soldiers. "Bring me the minstrel's harp," he said.

Soon the first soldiers came back with the knight's horse. The king was so happy that he jumped on the horse's back. "Giddap!" he shouted.

Now the horse did not like for someone else to ride him. He wanted the knight. So he threw the king off on the ground.

Just then the second soldiers came with the boy's dog. The king was so happy to see the dog who did tricks that he left the horse.

"Jump!" the king told the dog. But the dog would not do tricks for someone else. He wanted the boy.

"Lie down!" shouted the king. But the dog just looked at the king.

Then the third soldiers came up with the minstrel's harp. The king was so happy to see the beautiful harp that he left the dog.

He picked up the harp and ran his fingers over the strings. But it sounded awful. It was not at all like the music the minstrel played.

The king tried again. But this time it sounded even worse.

The king sat down to think. He had the knight's horse, the boy's dog, and the minstrel's harp, but he still didn't have everything.

The king thought and thought. Only the knight can ride the horse so well. Only the boy can get the dog to do his wonderful tricks. And only the minstrel can play the beautiful music on the harp.

Then the king had an idea. He took the knight's horse back to the knight. "I want to be your friend," said the king. "Would you ride your horse for me?"

"I would love to ride my horse for a friend," said the knight. So he rode his horse before the king. The king was so happy.

Then the king took the boy's dog back to him. "I want to be your friend," said the king. "Would you have your dog do some tricks for me?"

"Oh, yes," said the boy. "That would be fun to have him do tricks for a friend." So the boy had his dog do tricks for the king. The king was so happy.

Then the king took the harp back to the minstrel. "I want to be your friend," said the king. "Would you play something for me?"

"Yes," said the minstrel. "I would like to do that for a friend." So the minstrel played beautiful music for the king.

Each day after that the knight and the boy and the minstrel went to see the king. The king was always so happy to see them.

"Now I do have everything," said the king. "For I have good friends to make me happy."

David C. Cook

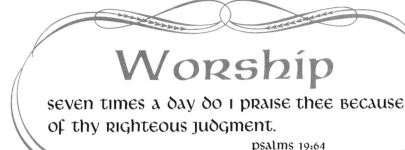

seven times a day do I praise thee because
of thy righteous judgment.

psalms 19:64

God's Magnificence

We are explorers more or less,
In life's uncharted wilderness,
So much remains for those to find,
Who have an open, eager mind.
A miracle beyond belief,
The fragile texture of a leaf—
No laboratory can produce
A snow-capped mountain green with spruce.

No chemist's beaker can contain
The crystal formula of rain,
You will not find a patent on
The coral ribbons of the dawn.
Say what you will, nobody knows
What truly makes a living rose,
In spite of all we've learned so far,
Man cannot duplicate a star!

The cool gray moss, the ivied vine,
Aren't rolled from an assembly line,
The palette of the artist holds
No match for autumn's reds and golds.
The greatest sonnet ever penned,
Is but an echo of the wind—
And all things past and all things hence,
. . . Attest to God's Magnificence!

Grace E. Easley

God's Way

There is a way that seemeth right unto a man,
But the end thereof are the ways of death.

God's Way is not the way of man.

Man, the blind molish creature,
Burrowing through black tunnels of cloying existence
His bleak markings
Full of the anguish of life,
Fuller of the horror of its end.
Desiring it,
Despising it,
Loving, clinging to it,
And with the same betraying breath,
Fleeing and hiding from it.
What more miserable creature than man,
Whose greatest comfort in life
Is its negation?
To whom joy is to dull the senses,
Blow his mind,
Overwhelm his consciousness in a flood of frantic sound,
That the call of Life be left unheard.
Need fully clinging to worldly clamor
Devised to deafen his very thoughts,
Lest he lose his mind
And unhap'ly come to the knowledge
That he had also
Lost his soul.
In the secret corridors of his spirit,
Divinely designed to be the abode of the Almighty,
There echo instead the vacuous walls of
Naught.
The only sound
The morbid reflections
Of irrational, ingrown thought.
See the ways of man,
Streaming in frantic flight
From haunted corridors of corrupting self,
Unbearable,
For in them walks man
In justified fear that God . . .
Might just be there.

See the way of man,
Justified by his superior mind,
As though that superior mind
Were designed for one purpose only:
To excuse the errant life.
What pitiful function for so noble a creation;
A mind, shaped in the image of God,
Employed in the pursuit
Of all else.

There is a way that seemeth right unto a man,
But the end thereof are the ways of death.

God's Way is not the way of man.

Abode a creature uncreated,
Shaped in the image of man,
Eternally God,
Mystery of infinite logic,
Incomprehensible,
Lest he be grasped.
Let man's computer brain comprehend,
Then willingly could he accept.
Thus is the way of man,
So dazzled he
By the brilliant shine of feeble logic,
So prided by plaudit of peers,
So deafened by chaotic noise
Of higher learning,
That the simple spirit,
Deprived of essential senses,
Gropes in errored ways,
Failing to see,
To touch,
To know,
The Way of God,
Everlasting Word,
Spoken by HIM,
Sent by HIM,
Fulfilled in HIM,
Standing,
ONE,
Unique in the Cosmos of man,
Hated of those
Who hate their very life.

Continued on page 130

Continued from page 129

Small wonder—
Hated—
For He is that very Life.
Such is the Way of God,
The Way,
Disdained by mortal feet,
That prefer to run the race of man,
Striving in vain to win the prize,
The prize that is gained
Only by him
Who runs not at all.
A prize? Never!
A gift? Ever!
A prize only to ONE
Who ran the Race of Death
And won life for all;
All those
Whose eyes do see,
Whose ears do hear,
Whose spirit dares believe,
Believing the unbelievable,
Trusting the impossible,
Seeking the One who finds.
Such was the Way of God,
A Way so tangible,
So true,
So real,
That men could grasp,
But only with hands,
To scourge,
Curse,
Revile,
And nail upon a cross.
Such is the Way of God,
Never the way of man.

There is a way that seemeth right unto a man,
But the end thereof are the ways of death.

God's Way is not the way of man.

Jerome Hines

✳ ✳

Blind

I cannot view the bloom upon the rose,
    But oh, the scent is very dear to me;
And I can feel the cooling breeze that blows
    Thro' pearl-tipped peaks of hills I cannot see.

I cannot see the wild birds on the wing,
    But I can hear the swallows in the eaves;
I hear the song that nature has to sing—
    The gentle music of the rustling leaves.

I cannot see the children going by,
    But I can hear their laughter as they pass;
I cannot see the sunset in the sky,
    But I can feel the swaying of the grass.

Author Unknown

Just A Moment Longer

Lord, I am confounded!
Your earth is too beautiful
To pass over lightly.
Let me pause to watch
The tide come in,
Let me linger to watch
The poinciana bloom.
Let me hold the puffs of silk cotton
Before they blow away.
Hold the fiery sun up
Just over the western waters
A moment longer,
Just a moment while I look again.
Let me hug this sleepy child
To my breast
A few more years,
A few more hours,
Just a moment more,
Lord.

Violet Munro

Night Symphony

There's a whispering song on the water
and wet shuffling sands where
twittering sandpipers call,
their tiny feet clattering
over rocks and shells as
they feed ever
seeking for
more.

A spring tide is moving tonight
and its rhythmical motion rocks
turbulent meadows of kelp in
their cradle of ocean while
a slender new moon tucked
in a basket of stars
floats over the
highways of
heaven to
regions
afar.

I think of the dawn of beginnings
those six mighty "days" when an
Infinite Voice set in motion
the earth, sea, and sky,
yes everything dwelling
therein then He said
"It is good." So I
kneel to the God
of creation.

Sue Boynton

GOLDEN THOUGHT

The true work of art is but the
shadow of divine perfection.

Michelangelo

Creation

Lord, You made such a lovely world,
I cannot understand
How men can scoff and ridicule,
And say it was not planned.

Each time I see the blue, blue sky,
The moon and stars above,
I know this world was made by You,
A token of Your love.

The wooded hills, the rippling brooks,
The flowers of every hue—
They could not have just happened, Lord.
They were designed by you.

The flaming sky at set of sun,
The trees, the fresh green grass,
The singing birds, yea, man himself
Did not just come to pass!

It could not be by accident,
The playful hand of fate;
This world could only have been made
By One who's very great!

Betty F. Anderson

God, Help Me Again

You made me, God—You gave me life . . . And I belong to You . . . And I should be obedient . . . In everything I do . . . Obedient to all Your laws . . . And grateful for Your grace . . . And for my daily strength to meet . . . The trials I must face . . . I do acknowledge You, My God . . . I worship on my knees. . . . I am Your own with heart and soul . . . My mind and memories . . . I know all this, my God, and yet . . . How sorry is my plight . . . Because so often what I do . . . Is wrong instead of right . . . Forgive me for my failures, God . . . And help me start anew. . .The kind of life on earth You want . . . To have me live for You.

James J. Metcalfe

GOLDEN THOUGHT

If I could hear Christ praying for me in the next room, I would not fear a million enemies. Yet distance makes no difference; He is praying for me.

Robert Murray McCheyne

Good Afternoon!

The sun has kissed each pansy's smiling face;
Has warmed these golden hours of day,
Come linger in the garden for a while
Before night's shadows dim our way.

The portulacas now are wide awake,
But soon again they all will doze;
The larkspur, gowned in Heaven's blue, stands tall
Beside the Princess Margaret Rose.

Our afternoon of life is golden too;
The morning's past, soon comes the night,
But we who follow Christ will have no fear,
For Jesus is our Guide, the Way and Light.

Esther B. Heins

Room For Me

The stable was small. Low was the wall.
Shepherds were there. Kings brought jewels rare.
Animals sleeping. Angels watch keeping,
But there's room in the stable for me.

The cross towered high. Soldiers stood by.
Mary kneeled there. Friends bowed in prayer.
Three mortals died. The heart of God cried.
But there's room at the Cross for me.

The streets are narrow; even the sparrow
Is counted in throngs. There are angels with songs.
Saints of all ages, apostles and sages.
But there's room in His house for me.

Lucille Crumley

Prayer

Prayer is the prelude to peace, the prologue to power, the preface to purpose, and the pathway to perfection.

William Arthur Ward

The Nazareth Shop

I wish I had been His apprentice, to see Him each morning at seven,
As He tossed His gray tunic far from Him, the Master of earth and of heaven;
When He lifted the lid of His work chest and opened His carpenter's kit,
And looked at the chisels and augers, and took the bright tools out of it;
While He gazed at the rising sun tinting the dew on the opening flowers,
And smiled as He thought of His Father, whose love floods this planet of ours;
When He fastened His apron about Him, and put on His workingman's cap;
And grasped the smooth haft of His hammer to give the bent woodwork a tap,
Saying, "Lad, let us finish this ox yoke. The farmer must put in his crop."
O, I wish I had been His apprentice, and worked in the Nazareth shop!

McIntyre

A Thirsty Soul

Waves sweep high;
   suffocation looms like descending dark.
I shrink from illogical movement,
   lest suffocation take dominion,
   and waves scale my desperate thirsty soul.
I drink of living water;
   the waves deplete.
I must drink daily, my soul's thirst a chasm.
Like Peter I cry, "Help."
   Christ stretches his hand to meet mine.
My soul's thirst for strength, peace, and joy is quenched,
Once again the waves deplete.

Twyla Wood

Golden Thought

When I think of God, my heart is so full of joy
that the notes leap and dance as they leave my
pen; and since God has given me a cheerful heart,
I serve him with a cheerful spirit.

Franz Joseph Haydn

The Hand Of God

On the outskirts of the desert where village life goes along much as it did centuries ago, an eclipse of the moon occurred. As the shadow crept across the face of the moon the residents were asked what was happening. Some replied that the moon was only sinking behind a mountain; others claimed it was merely the quarter phase of the moon; still others said it was hiding behind a cloud, but one old village sheikh, undisturbed by the growing darkness, imaginatively assured the onlookers that the phenomenon was the hand of God covering the moon. To be able to see the hand of God at work in the world is one of the greatest assets one can have. When the shadows are gathering for life's darker moments, the person who can still see God's hand at work, even in unfavorable circumstances, will be master of any situation life may impose upon him.

Paul S. McElroy

136

My Needs

Some days my needs are simple things—
A bird to cross my cloudless sky
And spread the color of his wings,
And leave a song as he goes by.

At other times I need a star—
One beam to pierce a long dark night;
Seems heaven's door is then ajar
And sending me a ray of light.

A silence often fills my need—
The silence of the falling snow,
A solitude, a book to read,
A time to learn things I should know.

Sometimes my need is daily bread,
Again my need is something more,
For I could feast and be half fed
Had I no spiritual food in store.

Oh, I have many sundry needs—
A woodland trail, the sun, the sod,
The hills, the fields, the plants and seeds,
But always, always I need God.

Johnielu Barber Bradford

In God's Hands

Having found that his own way has led him to failure, a man begins to think it possible that acceptance of God's way might bring him to a satisfying life after all. Having been too proud to stoop even to God, it may dawn on him that stooping to God might be the height of wisdom. God can dwell in humble hearts, but in no other. As soon as we have given in and know ourselves as very small creatures, our peace begins. And then we discover that God is the one great interest which can grow greater and more sufficient unto life's end. Our hope is in God, and our peace can never come to us till we forget self and leave ourselves in his hands.

A. Herbert Gray

The Greatest

The greatest ally is courage; the greatest partner is enthusiasm.
The greatest beauty is simplicity; the greatest power is love.
The greatest prosperity is health; the greatest fortune is friends.
The greatest truth is God; the greatest privilege is prayer.
The greatest success is service; the greatest joy is peace.
The greatest journey is faith; the greatest adventure is generosity.
The greatest teacher is experience; the greatest lesson is adversity.
The greatest preacher is patience; the greatest sermon is example.
The greatest habit is gratitude; the greatest gesture is forgiveness.
The greatest talent is endurance; the greatest discovery is light.
The greatest wisdom is integrity; the greatest blessing is freedom.
The greatest reality is spirit; the greatest miracle is rebirth.
The greatest path is unity; the greatest gift is Christ.

William Arthur Ward

A Prayer For Patience

God, teach me to be patient—
Teach me to go slow—
Teach me how to "wait on You"
When my way I do not know . . .
Teach me sweet forbearance
When things do not go right
So I remain unruffled
When others grow uptight . . .
Teach me how to quiet
My racing, rising heart
So I may hear the answer
You are trying to impart . . .
Teach me to LET GO, dear God,
And pray undisturbed until
My heart is filled with inner peace
And I learn to know YOUR WILL!

Helen Steiner Rice

GOLDEN VERSE

Those who put their faith
In things beyond the strength of man,
Wait with quiet confidence
The working of His plan.

Patience Strong

Peace Defined

Peace is one of the great words of the Holy Scriptures. Peace is the deepest and most universal desire of man. "Grant us Thy peace, Oh Lord," has been the prayer of all ages. It is the cry of the uneasy world today.

Nothing soothes and satisfies the heart like the sense of being loved. The little child who is tired from his play becomes suddenly frightened and runs to his mother. He is crying and she gathers her child in her arms, and quiets him with assuring words which mean, "I love you". Soon the child is contented and happy in the sense of being loved. He is at peace.

God is reaching out His arms, waiting to enfold us in the security of His peace. His love is ever present and waiting to be accepted by mankind. The peace of the Christian is in the knowledge of being Divinely loved. If we believe in Christ, as the Son of God, we are sure of a divine affection—deep, infinite and imperishable. We are sure because Jesus said, "For God so loved the world, that He gave His Only Begotten Son, that whosoever believeth on Him should not perish, but have everlasting life." The peace of God is the reward and the blessing, and the crown of life's effort, and the glory of eternity.

Peace is the knowledge of being forgiven. In every heart there is a consciousness of sin and guilt that makes man restless, dissatisfied, and unhappy. There is no cure, nor rest, or release from it, but to have it Divinely pardoned; and to have the separation from God ended and done away with. That is the peace offered to every man. We need it in this modern world more than ever before. No 'new era' will ever change its message or do away with its necessity.

Peace must begin in the soul of each individual. Peace will never come with a man-made treaty among nations, or a mass agreement of churches. It must begin with you and God, then spread out like a beam of light.

Lucille Crumley

His Eye Is On The Sparrow

I was a sparrow
trapped on a sunporch
battering myself
from pane to pane
frantic to be free.
At last I found Your door.

It had been open
all the time.

Terry Germain Free

The Church The Bible Built

Many years ago the Rev. Robert Burris, now 90 years of age, worked for four and one-half years as a missionary in South China. As part of his ministry he journeyed into the mountains carrying copies of the Scriptures in Chinese for distribution. In this way, although he could not speak fluent Chinese, the people were given God's Word. Toward the end of his term Mr. Burris and three companions began a 180-mile journey with 4,000 copies of the Chinese New Testament. In the first 10 days about half of these New Testaments had been distributed. Then, in the remote countryside, they were stopped by five armed bandits who took everything—money, clothing, shoes—and the remaining 2,000 copies of the New Testament. Mr. Burris and his friends limped home barefooted in their shirts and trousers, glad to be alive.

Approximately 25 years later when Mr. Burris was the pastor of a church in Ohio, he and his wife attended a lecture with slides presented by a missionary to South China. Among the slides shown was a picture of the very place in which he had been robbed by the bandits. "Now," the missionary said, "we come to the most important slide in my collection. I call it The Miracle Church." The picture on the screen showed a large rough empty building. "This is The Miracle Church," the missionary continued, "because no one knows who started it, or how. Every Sunday, 400 people attend, each with a copy of the New Testament in Chinese. No one knows where they got these New Testaments. So far as is known, no missionary or distributor ever went into these mountains which are infested with bandits and robbers. Yet today, the church is there and the people have God's Word."

Mr. Burris smiled in gratitude. God's Word, taken from him that day by the bandits had been building its own church in China for 25 years.

Author Unknown

What Jesus Did For Me

A young Roman had been condemned to death for treason. An elder brother, who had lost both of his arms while serving in his country's wars, stepped up before the judges, holding up the stumps of his two arms, and pleaded for his brother's life, not for what his brother had done, but for what he had done. He confessed that his brother was guilty; he confessed that his brother was worthy of death; but for what he had done in the service of his country, he pleaded that his brother's life might be spared. And looking on what the brother had done, the judges for his sake pardoned the guilty brother. That is just what Christ does for sinners. Christ died on Calvary that we might live. We deserved death, but for the sake of Christ, and because He laid down His life that we might live, God pardons our sins.

Author Unknown

True Goal

No leaf is like another one.
Each has uniqueness of design—
Some variance in shades of green,
A difference in edging's line.
No bird wing is a duplicate.
Each has a pattern all its own,
Its individual coloring;
Each stands distinctive and alone.
This shell is an original;
This stone is shaped one certain way.
Tomorrow's dawn will never be
Exactly like the one today.
And so it is with man. Each one
Has his own talents, great and small,
And makes his contribution to
The common good, the wealth of all.
Lord, have Your way with me, so I
Become that rare and special soul
That You have destined me to be.
Lord, help me reach my one, true goal!

Marie Daerr

Glory

Hold close the glory that touches your life,
The rare moment in which you hold your breath
Awestruck by that something beyond—

The glory of the indescribable changing colors
    of the sunset;
The glory of that delicate moment when the rose
    reaches its perfection;
The glory and satisfaction of a difficult goal
    achieved;
The glory of the rare moments when friendship
    is touched with true understanding;
The glory of the deep feeling of oneness between
    yourself and a loved one;
The greatest glory of all — knowing that you are
    a part of the eternal plan of God!

Nelia M. Dosser

A Prayer

Let me do my work each day; and if the darkened hours of despair overcome me, may I not forget the strength that comforted me in the desolation of other times. May I still remember the bright hours that found me walking over the silent hills of my childhood, or dreaming on the margin of the quiet river, when a light glowed within me, and I promised God to have courage amid the tempests of the changing years. Spare me from bitterness and from the sharp passions of unguarded moments.

May I not forget that poverty and riches are of the Spirit. Though the world know me not, may my thoughts and actions be such as shall keep me friendly with myself. Lift my eyes from the earth, and let me not forget the uses of the stars. Forbid that I should judge others lest I condemn myself.

Let me not follow the clamor of the world, but walk calmly in my path. Give me a few friends who will love me for what I am; and keep ever burning before my vagrant steps the kindly light of hope. And though age and infirmity overtake me, and I come not within sight of the castle of my dreams, teach me still to be thankful for life, and for time's olden memories that are good and sweet; and may the evening's twilight find me gentle still.

Max Ehrmann

Christmas

thanks be unto God for his
unspeakable gift.

II CORINTHIANS 6:2

At Christmas

A man is at his finest towards the finish of the year;
    He is almost what he should be when the Christmas season's here;
Then he's thinking more of others than he's thought the months before,
    And the laughter of his children is a joy worth toiling for.
He is less a selfish creature than at any other time;
    When the Christmas spirit rules him he comes close to the sublime.

When it's Christmas man is bigger and is better in his part;
    He is keener for the service that is prompted by the heart.
All the petty thoughts and narrow seem to vanish for awhile
    And the true reward he's seeking is the glory of a smile.
Then for others he is toiling and somehow it seems to me
    That at Christmas he is almost what God wanted him to be.

If I had to paint a picture of a man I think I'd wait
    Till he'd fought his selfish battles and had put aside his hate.
I'd not catch him at his labors when his thoughts are all of self,
    On the long days and the dreary when he's striving for himself.
I'd not take him when he's sneering, when he's scornful or depressed,
    But I'd look for him at Christmas when he's shining at his best.

Man is ever in a struggle and he's oft misunderstood;
    There are days the worst that's in him is the master of the good,
But at Christmas kindness rules him and he puts himself aside
    And his petty hates are vanquished and his heart is opened wide.
Oh, I don't know how to say it, but it seems to me
    That at Christmas man is almost what God sent him here to be.

Edgar A. Guest

The Gift

The gift to be true, must be the flowering of the giver unto me, correspondent to my flowing unto him.

Emerson

The Paper Flowers

In a makeshift vase in my small living room are some paper flowers—obviously homemade. Each time I look at them they remind me of how very fortunate I am.

It was just before Christmas a year ago when they knocked on my door—a small boy and girl, each clutching a handful of homemade paper flowers. The children were bundled in clothes which looked as if they had had many previous owners.

A cold, raw wind was blowing. The noses of the two were red under their faded woolen caps. But it was their eyes which held my attention—pleading eyes. One of them spoke: "Flowers, lady?"

I looked at the "flowers"—soiled, bent and crudely made by little fingers unaccustomed to making such things. I smiled, and saw the immediate look of hurt in the small one's eyes. "They're very pretty," I added quickly. *"That's* why I was smiling."

Another blast of wind whipped around us. "Won't you come in," I asked, "and have a cup of hot cocoa?" They looked at one another for a moment and then stepped inside.

I brought the cocoa in a pan, gave each a cup and saucer, then poured. They sipped the hot drink silently. And then the little boy spoke: "Lady—are you *rich?*" I had to laugh. "Me? Rich? Heavens, no! What ever gave you that idea?"

He stared down at his cocoa. "Your cups and saucers—they match." Matching cups and saucers—my man with a good job—a modest home—furniture shabby, but comfortable—food in the icebox.

I had never before realized how rich I was.

I bought their flowers—all of them, and kissed the two as they left. They never knew how *very* much they had given me.

M. Buxbaum

How Far To Bethlehem?

How far is it to Bethlehem?
  How steep the way and long
Before we hear as shepherd heard
  That glorious angel song?

How far is it to Bethlehem?
  How dark the way and wild
Until we kneel before a crib
  Worshipping the Child?

O tell us of our pilgrimage.
  How many miles? How far?
Until our eyes behold the sign,
  The radiance of a star.

Then suddenly the answer comes
  Renewed with faith each year.
To each of us with open heart
  Bethlehem is *here!*

Jean Conder Soule

Jesus

Tenderly Joseph watched
his lovely Mary,
remembering angel words:
"He shall save
His people
from their sins".
With reverent voice
he spoke,
"His name is Jesus."

Love and wonder
shone in her eyes
as she held him,
this promised child.
Softly she whispered,
"Jesus."

Leota Campbell

Everywhere, Everywhere—
Christmas!

Now at this season of the birth of Jesus, the world draws closer together—linked by the common bonds of joy and faith and goodwill. In lands of palm and pine, of jungle, veldt, and tundra, the faces of many shades of skin light up at the mention of Christmas, and voices in innumerable languages sing praises to the Father of all and to His Son, the Babe of Bethlehem.

Esther Baldwin York

Find The Star

If I could find the star that shown
   the night that Christ was born
Would its bright light reflect a path
   to banish hate and scorn?

If I could call the shepherds back
   that heard the angel's voice,
Would they in some unusual way
   help mankind all rejoice?

If I could locate wisemen three,
   that traveled from the east,
Would they explain with hearts aglow,
   why the best of us are least?

If I could hear the heavenly hosts
   that sang so long ago,
Would they express a praise in song,
   of love we all could know?

Of course these thoughts are fantasy,
   or at least a task too hard;
But there is a bright and shining star,
   we call Him Christ our Lord.

Joe A. Harris

God's Gifts

Not a lofty
evergreen
bejeweled with lights,
costly gifts
beneath;
but a tree
stripped of its branches
made into a cross
stark, ugly
makes known God's love.
Gifts beneath: joy,
peace, forgiveness,
Life eternal.
Come . . . Receive . . .

Leota Campbell

The Christmas Candle

This silver candle I shall light
And place upon my windowsill.
Its soft gold flame may help to cheer
A lone wayfarer on the hill.

It may lead someone to my door,
Someone discouraged, down the way,
And I shall bid him come and sup
And share my loaf this Christmas Day.

I cannot give my Lord and King
The gifts wise men brought Him of old;
But He will love this candle flame
As much, or more, than costly gold!

And oh, if this tall candle leads
One homeless, who seeks warmth and bed,
I shall invite him in, for he
Might be the dear Christ Child instead.

William Arnette Wofford

Christmas Miracle

With heavy heart I listened
As carolers sang out,
Rebelling at the words
Of peace and joy they sang about.

For me there was no peace, no joy,
No sense of Christmas cheer;
My saddened heart so filled with pain
And loneliness and fear.

And then, through tear-filled eyes I saw
The Christmas Star on high,
A star my tears had softened
To a cross there in the sky.

A cross—the symbol of God's love,
Shone through my grief and loss.
Had I not known the tears,
I might have never seen the cross.

Miraculously then, I felt
A sense of sweet release,
And, gratefully, my heart received
The wonder of His peace.

Helen Lowrie Marshall

GOLDEN VERSE

When Christmas passes, as it will,
May gladness linger with you still;
May friends be true the whole year through,
And all things good abide with you.

Author Unknown

The Innkeeper's Lament

"I did not know! How could I have known?" The speaker was an old man in his late sixties. His long, white beard fell heavily upon his sunken chest, while burning eyes peered out from under shaggy, gray brows. His voice of protest rose to the high-pitched whine of one who had had one chance, and one only, to gain historical immortality—and had dropped that chance.

"How could I have known?" His burning eyes challenged the ring of listeners that had gathered round him as he began his story. Some of them could not have been in the world when he made his tragic mistake as Bethlehem's only innkeeper.

No one felt called upon to reply. And the old one dropped his head a moment in silent reminiscence. When he spoke again the whining challenge was gone from his voice, and he spoke wearily, as a man very tired from wrestling with a problem to which he could find no solution.

"There I was," he explained, perhaps for the thousandth time, "with the whole responsibility of entertaining Caesar's officers who had come to Bethlehem to enroll the children of David. Not only did I have Malchus, whom Augustus had sent to us with his retinue, but there was Jonas, the rich man of Tiberias who had come to be enrolled at the place of his nativity; and there were men from the palace with their ladies. They filled the inn. Even the servants were turned out of their quarters to make room for some of the poorer guests. Then came this Joseph with his girl-wife. I had eyes. I could see her state. I knew that she needed a room and a bed, but what could I do? Could I tell my lord Malchus to go to the stalls of the cave? Could I tell Jonas to go sleep with the cattle? Did I not have the reputation of the inn to think of? Besides, I could not know who they were!"

Again his voice trailed into silence. Finally, he spoke again. "You see, they went to the cave when I told them there was no room in the inn. Perhaps I did speak shortly to them, for I had been sorely tried, what with the great guests demanding this and that, and the ever-increasing crowds clamoring for comforts that I did not have to offer.

"I could not know that her time was so near upon her. How could I have known? And if I had known, what could I have done? The inn was full. I had no room." His hands spread out before them, pleading for understanding.

"I saw a dim light in the mouth of the cave that night when I went out to shut the gate. I saw shadowy movements out there again when I arose at midnight. Somehow, I could not sleep. I was nervous and excited from the strain of the day before. Finally, I saw men coming down out of the hills, and in the light of the full moon, I recognized

Continued on page 152

Continued from page 151

shepherds approaching the cave. I was startled, I went outside and approached the cave, and then it was that I saw the strangest sight of my life. By the light of the flickering torch that burned inside the cave, I saw the man Joseph standing silently by, his rugged features lit with emotion. On a bed of straw lay the wife, her face showing mingled pain and joy, while in a manger just above her lay a baby newborn. But strangest of all strange sights, I saw those shepherds from the hills kneeling by that manger as if they were worshiping God.

"When they arose at last and started to leave, I stepped back into the shadows and waited for them to go by. I heard one say to the others, 'Let us hasten away and tell the wonderful things that we have seen.'

" 'Yes,' said another. 'We have heard and seen angels this night.' For a moment they were still, and one said, 'Yes, and we have seen One greater than angels. We have seen the Babe and have worshiped Him.'

"Of course, I could not know what they meant, and although I went back to my bed, I did not sleep.

"As time passed I forgot the baby and his strange parents. Then when I was old and my son had taken over the inn to run it, I went up to Capernaum to visit a kinsman whom I had not seen for a long time. On the street one day I saw a throng of people, and passing close I saw her. Thirty years had passed since I had looked upon that face, but I knew it, still beautiful with the purity of motherhood, still half-sad and half-joyful, and by her side was a strong young man of striking countenance and the gracious bearing of a prince. I heard them say that He was her son, and I needed to hear no more. I knew that He was the babe that had slept in my cave the first night He spent upon earth, because I had turned His mother away from my door, for there was no room in the inn.

"Suddenly, He looked upon me and I shrank back, guilty, afraid. I thought He knew me, that He was going to point a finger at me and accuse me of committing a terrible sin that night. But just then a man rushed up to Him and cried, 'Lord, I will follow thee whithersoever thou goest!'

"He looked at the man, a little smile of indulgence on His face, and when He opened His mouth to speak, it was as though He were speaking to me. He said, 'The foxes have holes, and the birds of the air have nests; but the Son of man hath not where to lay his head.'

"I could not stand it. Though I knew He had answered another man, I knew, too, that I was the first to turn Him out. Before I knew my mouth was open, my voice crying, 'Lord, have mercy and forgive!'

"Then He turned His eyes full upon me, and as if He understood what was in my heart, He answered, 'Thy sins are forgiven thee. Go, and sin no more.'

"I never forgot Him or those words that He spoke to me, although I never saw Him again until three days ago. I said to my firstborn that I would go to Jerusalem for the feast of the Passover. So the next day at an early hour my son took me up to Jerusalem. Now, I almost wish that I had never gone.

"I saw Him again. They were driving Him out of the city, and on His shoulder was a heavy wooden cross. My heart flamed at the injustice of their treatment of Him, and then He turned and looked at me. As I looked into His eyes for the second time, my heart smote me with sorrow at the memory of the time that I turned His mother from my door. O God! That I should have been the first to drive Him out!

"They tell me that they killed Him at the place of the skull, that there He died on the cross He bore when I saw Him. And now He is dead. Never again will He apply to me for shelter. Never can I redeem the opportunity that I lost over thirty years ago. It might have been in my house where He first saw the light of life. But no; it was in my cave. The rude, uncultured shepherds of the hills were there before I reached Him. They will be remembered long after I have been forgotten. And then the men (Magi they are called) that came from the Gentiles and worshiped before Him will be named in connection with His birth after I, a son of Israel, am forgotten. So my stable is more honored than my home. The manger will be held in sacred memory instead of a bed in my house. Shepherds will have their names mentioned in song, and strangers from the Gentiles will be lauded for their faith, while I, Hillel, the innkeeper of Bethlehem, will be remembered in cold scorn because there was no room in my inn. Yea, the very cattle of my stalls hold a place in the heart of Israel that I covet this day."

He was quiet so long that his audience thought he slept. But, finally he opened his eyes again and spoke.

"They tell me" (his voice a husky whisper now) "that He promised to rise from the dead; even now the city is filled with rumors. If He is risen, do you suppose that I, who turned Him and His mother away that night, might get to see Him just once more?"

The innkeeper was so full of his lament that he did not notice the young man who had joined the listeners. The old man felt him before he saw him. He cried out urgently, "I did not know! I never would have driven Him out if I had known!" The stranger smiled and nodded His head that He understood and turned to go. The old man's head jerked up, his burning eyes boring into the back of the young man. His mouth opened, his thin lips framing a name. Then his husky voice sounded a note of joy. He had hardly got the name out of his mouth when Mary's Son was gone!

Author Unknown

The Wisest Of The Wise

I'll stand beside the keeper of the inn,
Challenging those who charge him with the sin
That let the Child be born within his stable.
I say he did the best that he was able,
Under the circumstance. Where else would there
Be privacy and summer-scented air?
The beasts, benign in their nobility,
Stood watch; and this, at least it seems to me,
Gave courtesy unto the act of birth.
The hostel must have reeled with raucous mirth,
Jangling the laden night with feast and dance
As Roman taxes found the dice of chance.
Only a wise man would have seen the manger
As a cradle beyond the pry of stranger.
When pompous fingers shame his guiltless deed,
I'm on his side, disciple of the need
To say he was the wisest one of all,
Providing the sanctuary of the stall.

Ralph W. Seager

Bright Fragment

I think that someone led me
Down the long, cold hall,
With a lamp held high—
Someone tall.

Were there others in the parlor?
I only saw the tree
With countless candles burning
And a doll, in pink, for me;

And there were shining colored balls
I could see my picture in
With a funny bulgy forehead
And no chin.
The fir tree had a spicy smell,
There was candy—warmth and light—
And someone singing, singing
Of a silent, holy night.

Theodosia Benjamin

Bethlehem

Bethlehem?
An inn's stable?
The Savior of the world?
Why Bethlehem?
My mind rebelling questioned
until the Light of the world
shone upon the dark and secret
recesses of my own heart
and I saw why Bethlehem
why hell, why the cross
why the empty tomb
why God became man
for me.

Dorothy I. Buitendyk

Christmas Peace

A shining rainbow arched above
　　The planet earth tonight,
Illumined by the Star of Love,
　　The Holy Christmas Light;
The magic span invisible
　　Unites the hearts of men,
And the sound of angel music
　　Floats down to earth again:

Peace on the earth, goodwill to all,
　　We hear the sweet refrain,
It makes the troubled heart rejoice
　　And brings surcease to pain;
Oh, Holy One, put out the flame
　　Of hate that burns so bright,
And in its ashes plant Thy Rose
　　Of Christmas Peace tonight!

Dorothy M. Cahoon

GOLDEN THOUGHT

It is good to be children sometimes, and never better than at Christmas, when its mighty Founder was a child Himself.

Charles Dickens

A Special Christmas Gift

Jamie vaulted quickly from the wagon when Pa reined the horses to a stop in the frontier settlement of New Town. His older brother and sister, Paul and Hester, climbed down to stand beside him. This would be their last trip into town before Christmas and their last chance to buy gifts.

"Be back in an hour," Pa said, tying the team. "Hear?"

"Yes, sir," Jamie was the first to answer. He knew Pa was worried about leaving Ma at the farm with only Mrs. Fowler to look after her, even though Ma had said over and over that she would be all right.

"You are not to hurry," she had spoken from the wide bed which was pulled close to the bedroom window so she could see out. Then she had smiled so sweetly that her whole face lighted up. Just remembering her made Jamie feel warm inside. He knew Ma was about the bravest woman in the world. She hadn't complained a single time since the accident. Jamie shivered. How frightened he and his brother and sister had been when, soon after Pa and Ma had started for town one morning, Pa had come limping home, carrying Ma. Ma's face had been white with pain, but even then she had smiled.

"Team bolted, and the wagon overturned," Pa had explained briefly and sent Paul for the doctor.

After Ma had found out that she would have to spend several months in bed, her only worry was it made more work for everyone.

Jamie's fingers closed about the coins in his pocket as he followed Paul and Hester into Wilson's Emporium. He wished he had more money. He wanted to buy a wonderful, shining gift for Ma this year.

Mr. Wilson stood behind the counter, turning a key around and around in the side of a small box. "Morning," he said. Then he placed the box on the counter and smiled when a tinkly tune sounded and two tiny figures on top of the box turned in a slow circle.

"A music box!" Jamie breathed, his eyes wide. He turned to Hester and Paul, "Like Ma had when she was a little girl. She told us about it, remember? Only hers was shaped like a tiny house and had a little girl on top—a girl in a blue dress."

Hester and Paul nodded, and Jamie turned eagerly back to Mr. Wilson. This was the shining gift for Ma! But when Mr. Wilson quoted the price, Jamie's eyes opened wide. He had never seen that much money in his whole life!

How sweet it sounded, Jamie thought, like a bird's song. How Ma would love it! Suddenly, an idea popped into his head. He would make Ma a music box for Christmas—a special kind of music box. Jamie was good at making things. Everyone was always bragging about the animals he whittled out of the scraps of seasoned walnut Pa saved for him.

While Hester and Paul selected their gifts, Jamie wandered about the store, studying the shelves. Mr. Wilson finally came over to wait on him.

"Now, Jamie, what can I do for you?"

Jamie pointed to three small cans of paint, a brush, and a box of wood-working tools. He heard Hester catch her breath in disapproval.

"You're supposed to buy a gift for Ma, not for yourself," she whispered angrily.

"I'm going to use these to make Ma's gift," Jamie said.

"Humph!" said Hester, tossing her head.

"Some excuse!" Paul grinned. "You've been wanting some wood-working tools for a long time, Jamie."

"Wait! Just you wait until Christmas!" Jamie cried. His heart sank when he saw that neither Hester nor Paul believed him.

Pa was waiting at the wagon. "Did you find nice gifts for Ma?" he asked.

"Paul and I did," Hester said, "but Jamie—"

"Leave Jamie alone, Sis," Paul interrupted. "He's just a kid."

Jamie climbed into the wagon. He wanted to explain that he was going to make a music box like the one Ma used to have, but he knew they would laugh and tease. He'd show them!

From then on Jamie spent every free moment working on his mother's Christmas gift. The tiny house was easy to make, but carving the little girl with outstretched arms was so difficult that more than once he almost gave up. He started several and discarded them. Finally, he finished one and decided it would do.

Paul and Hester were curious, but Jamie worked in secret and kept his gift well hidden. At long last it was finished and painted.

Continued on page 158

Continued from page 157

Jamie was up at dawn on Christmas morning. He filled the small house with grain that trickled through an opening onto the small railed porch. Later, when Pa was carrying Ma to the couch in the living room, Jamie ran outside to hang the music box in the big oak tree outside Ma's window. When he hurried back inside, Pa had already lighted the candles on the Christmas tree, and he was waiting to call out the names on the packaged gifts.

Everyone laughed and chattered as they opened their gifts, and Jamie was too excited about his new sled and a big box of modeling clay to worry about what Ma would think of a music box that wouldn't play.

"Where's your gift for Ma, Jamie?" Hester cried, after all the packages were opened.

"Come to Ma's room," Jamie said. His heart was in his throat as he ran ahead to stand at the window. Hanging from a limb on the tree outside, the small yellow house swayed gently, and the carved figure of the little girl in blue seemed almost alive.

Jamie heard the others come in, heard the creak of bedsprings as Pa gently deposited Ma on the bed.

"Look!" Hester cried. "It's a little house. How pretty!"

As Jamie waited for his mother to speak, a cardinal fluttered down, perched on the porch of the tiny house and pecked at the grain.

"It's a bird feeder!" Paul cried.

Then Ma spoke. "No," she said softly. "It's more—it's a music box like the one I had when I was a little girl."

Jamie whirled around. "You remembered, Ma!" he cried happily, then he added, "I—I'm sorry I couldn't make it play."

"But it does!" Mother cried. "Listen!"

The cardinal lifted his head and sang, "Whoit, whoit, cheer - cheer - cheer!"

Suddenly, everyone was laughing, but it was warm, happy laughter, and Jamie's was the happiest of all.

Bernadine Beatie

A Children's Hymn

I think when I read that sweet story of old,
    When Jesus was here among men,
How he called little children as lambs to his fold,
    I should like to have been with him then.

Author Unknown

Why The Christmas Bells Rang

Many years ago in a far-off country there was a famous church with amazing bells in the church tower.

These amazing bells were known all over the globe for the rare beauty of their chimes. It was said that their sound was the sweetest melody in all the world. Because the music of the bells was so wonderful, they rang only on Christmas, never on ordinary occasions. And so it became the custom in that country for people to come from everywhere on Christmas Eve to the great church with its glorious Christmas bells. They would bring generous offerings and lay them upon the altar. It was only at this moment of sacrificial giving that the Christmas bells would be heard. Who rang them, no one knew. It was said that mysterious, angelic hands pulled the bell rope and the lovely sound would float out filling the air with melody until the church was engulfed in entrancing beauty.

Strangely enough, however, despite the great reputation of the bells and their music, probably no living soul had ever heard them. Their lovely sound was known only by tradition, because for long years the bells had not rung. This was due, so it was said, to the fact that the people had become neglectful of the church and indifferent to God. The gift offerings were growing smaller, and none had recently been great enough to cause the bells to ring. And so their beauty was remembered only as fathers had handed down the story to their children. Only in memory did their wonder remain.

Eventually this situation became something of a national scandal, and the king himself took the question in hand. He decided one Christmas that everyone should be encouraged to bring to the church the best and most generous gifts they could find. The king said that he would personally bring his own gift to the church on Christmas Eve. Naturally, everyone planned to visit the city for this great event.

Continued on page 160

Continued from page 159

No one made plans more carefully than two little boys who lived a long distance in the country. These two children were sons of a poor family, but somehow each managed to earn and save a small silver coin for an offering. Early on the afternoon before Christmas, holding the coins tightly so they would not be lost, they started their long walk to the city.

It was bitterly cold, and they had not gone very far before it started to snow heavily. But they did not let that stop them and, hand in hand, their shabby clothes wrapped tightly about them, they trudged on through the snow. Evening was coming on and it was growing dark, but they could see throngs hurrying to church.

Suddenly, the older boy stumbled on a dark object huddled in the snow. Kneeling down to investigate, he was startled to find an old woman, half frozen, but still alive. He lifted her and began to rub her wrists and temples. The woman's breathing grew more regular and he redoubled his efforts. As the boy worked at his task of human love and service, the lights of the city streets came on and immense crowds could be seen converging toward the church. The older boy looked up at his brother. "You go on to church," he said, handing him his treasured bit of silver. "Here's my offering. I must stay and do what I can to help this poor woman."

Reluctantly, the younger boy set off alone, the two small pieces of silver clutched in his hand. When he reached the church it was very crowded and the ceremony had started. Being small of stature, he managed to squeeze his way through the crowd to find a place near the front where he could see everything.

People were already beginning to bring their gifts to the altar. The gifts grew richer and more impressive and more luxurious as time passed. But the bells remained silent. Finally the king himself stood at the altar, resplendent in his magnificent robes and jewelry of state. With a dramatic gesture, he took his gold crown from his head and placed it on the altar. Everyone waited expectantly. Surely the bells would ring for this munificent and sacrificial gift. But not a sound was heard!

Sadly, the king turned to walk down the aisle and leave the church. The people began to follow him. Then, suddenly, from somewhere high in the vaulted arches of the church, the most heavenly music began to ring out. The tumultuous sound of the glorious Christmas bells filled the frosty air. The huge crowd stood transfixed. Then everyone looked back at the altar, but there was no one there.

No one, that is, but a small boy, shyly putting two tiny silver coins on the altar near the king's crown.

Raymond MacDonald Alden

Heaven

and the Lord shall deliver me from every evil work, and will preserve me unto his heavenly kingdom.

2 Timothy 4:18

At Last

When on my day of life the night is falling,
    And, in the winds from unsunned spaces blown,
I hear far voices out of darkness calling
    My feet to paths unknown,

Thou who hast made my home of life so pleasant,
    Leave not its tenant when its walls decay;
O Love Divine, O Helper ever-present,
    Be Thou my strength and stay!

Be near me when all else is from me drifting;
    Earth, sky, home's pictures, days of shade and shine,
And kindly faces to my own uplifting
    The love which answers mine.

I have but Thee, my Father! let Thy spirit
    Be with me then to comfort and uphold;
No gate of pearl, no branch of palm I merit,
    Nor street of shining gold.

Suffice it if — my good and ill unreckoned,
    And both forgiven through Thy abounding grace—
I find myself by hands familiar beckoned
    Unto my fitting place.

John Greenleaf Whittier

Understanding

Let me see his face again
Let me touch his hand,
Let me hear him say again!
"Dear, I understand."

You know how very lonely
A loving heart can be.
You know, too, of the longing
For a loved one's face to see.

We shared so much together
Throughout our many years,
Of work, and joy and laughter,
Cemented by some tears,

That days alone seem endless,
Each night a century long,
If you could just be home again,
Back where you belong!

Our home was not a castle
But we were happy there,
Life gave us many blessings
And so much love to share.

But he has gone to a fairer land
From which there's no return,
While I remain, until God calls,
To think, to dream, to yearn.

Rhena S. LaFever

The One Remains

The One remains, the many change and pass;
Heaven's light forever shines, Earth's shadows fly;
Life, like a dome of many-colored glass,
Stains the white radiance of Eternity . . .

John Keats
From "Adonais"

golden thought

I came from God, and I'm going back to God,
and I won't have any gaps of death in the middle
of my life.

George MacDonald

Thoughts On A Sunset

I watched the flaming orange ball
Sink slowly in the west,
The sky alight with color
As God put the earth to rest.

The lavenders, the pinks, the blues,
The scarlet and the gold—
I caught my breath in wonder
Such beauty to behold!

I thought of how the Psalmist says
The heavens declare God's glory;
And yet, I thought, they could not half
Begin to tell the story.

God shows Himself in nature, true,
A God of power and might;
One who rules the universe
And changes day to night;

And yet He fully shows Himself
Through Jesus Christ, His Son—
A God of love who gave His best
That our souls might be won.

So when I see a sunset,
Majestic though it be,
I thank my God for sending Christ
To show His love to me!

Betty Anderson

The Light On The Farthest Hills

Though the valley be dark with shadows,
And hushed be the singing rills,
O Heart, behold in the distance,
The light on the farthest hills.

The light! the light you are seeking!
Lift up your tired eyes
And glimpse it beyond the hilltops:
The blue of the clearing skies.

Let us forget the valley
And the long road that we came,
Let us move out and upward
Toward that golden flame.

Oh, let us leave behind us
The doubt, the fear and the dread:
There is God's glorious promise;
The light on the hills ahead!

Grace Noll Crowell

GOLDEN NUGGET

Winter is on my head but eternal spring is in my heart; I breathe at this hour the fragrance of the lilacs, the violets and the roses, just as twenty years ago. The nearer I approach the end, the plainer I hear around the immortal symphonies of the worlds which invite me.

Victor Hugo

I Trust You God

I trust You God to care
In death, the same as birth.
Your love cannot so change
Because this is Your earth.

Because You paint the rainbow
And tint the willow green,
You will gently draw the veil
That opens wide our world's between.

Lucille Crumley

One World

I raised my eyes aloft, and I beheld
The scattered chapters of the Universe
Gathered and bound into a single book
By the austere and tender hand of God.

Dante Alighieri, 1265-1321
From "The Divine Comedy"

A Parable of Life

Passengers below the deck
Huddled as the ship,
Storm-tossed, made them afraid
They'd not survive the trip.
Yet one lad in their midst
Courageous, though quite small,
Climbed back on deck as if
He weren't afraid at all.
Soon he returned and smiled,
"The Captain's my Father, you see.
We need not be afraid.
The Captain just smiled at me."

Perry Tanksley

"The Heavens Declare
The Glory Of God"

*"The heavens declare the glory of God; and the
firmament showeth His handiwork. Day unto day
uttereth speech, and night unto night showeth
knowledge." Psalm 19:1, 2.*

As we study the sun, moon, and stars and other heavenly bodies, we
are filled with awe and humility and adoration. On a clear moonlit
night, if we take time to look off into space and observe the planets
and the thousands of stars that are visible, we cannot but think of the
majesty, the greatness, the omnipotence, of the God who has made the
universe and who keeps these heavenly bodies moving in their courses
with absolute precision. In our childhood we think of these heavenly
bodies merely as twinkling stars, but with giant telescopes scientists
have found these stars to be worlds and suns similar to our own.

> I raised my eyes aloft, and beheld
> The scattered chapters of the universe
> Gathered and bound into a single book
> By the austere and tender hand of God.
>
> *Dante*

When telescopes were invented, and then perfected, astronomers
found so many, many heavenly bodies that they were hard put to
name or number them. Our finite minds cannot grasp the immen-
sity of the heavens. The size of our own planetary system is staggering.
Our mighty sun, though millions of miles away, is one of a group of
perhaps a hundred billion stars.

Dr. Harlow Shapley once referred to our world as a "little gob
of earth, with its splash of ocean, wisp of atmosphere, and smear of
biology." Our great solar system is just a tiny speck or particle in the
great Milky Way. When we try to understand our own world, our
minds are incapable of comprehending it all. But when we try to
think of the universe our minds are stunned. We seem to have had
a partial anesthetic—we just cannot fathom it. No wonder the
psalmist asked, "What is man, that Thou are mindful of him? and the
son of man, that Thou visitest him?" Psalm 8:4. At best, we are a
very, very small part of God's great universe.

When we stand on the deck of a steamer in mid-ocean, or walk
amidst the towering peaks of mighty mountain ranges, we feel our

insignificance. But when we think of our great solar system, we feel even more dwarfed in size. We might use the mile as a measuring rod. It is about 240,000 miles to the moon, and 93,000,000 miles to the sun. Our earth is a small part of our solar system, and our solar system is a very small part of the giant galaxy, and the galaxy a tiny part of God's great universe.

Astronomers, in trying to tell us the size of the universe, cannot even think of miles. The light-year is used as a measure. Light travels at a speed of 186,000 miles a second. Rays from the sun reach our world in about eight and a half minutes. It takes thirty-three years for light to reach us from Arcturus. Light which now reaches our planet from the fiery cluster of the suns of Hercules left that cluster about 34,000 years ago, traveling at 11,000,000 miles a minute. Light from the Andromeda Nebula travels 750,000 years before it reaches the earth. Truly, "the heavens declare the glory of God; and the firmament showeth His handiwork."

Author Unknown

Answers

I don't know all the answers,
Perhaps I'll never see
The reason You have chosen
This particular path for me.

So let me walk serenely,
For some happy day I'll find
All my questions answered
If I keep my hand in Thine.

Rhena S. LaFever

Hurrying Years

For life seems so little when life is past,
And the memories of sorrow flee so fast,
And the woes which were bitter to you and to me,
Shall vanish as raindrops which fall in the sea;
And all that has hurt us shall be made good,
And the puzzles which hindered be understood,
And the long, hard march through the
    wilderness bare
Seem but a day's journey when once we are there.

Susan Coolidge

Wings Against The Sun

Forever earthbound are my feet
Upon the rocky road ahead,
But high among the clouds, my thoughts,
And so my heart is comforted.
And if one shoulder aches, I shift
The burden to the other side,
Remembering the times I've laughed,
And not the ones in which I've cried.
Too short indeed the precious years,
To let a dream die needlessly,
Beyond tomorrow there awaits
A time and place designed for me.
And old hopes rising one by one,
—Are golden wings against the sun.

Grace E. Easley

Heaven Revisited

There are geographical problems connected with heaven. There are physical problems and chronological problems and environmental problems and problems relating to activity and growth. Because of these unresolved questions many men down the centuries have chosen to give the idea of heaven rather sorry treatment. Other men have used heaven to exploit their fellows by denying to them a decent living and then promising "pie in the sky when you die." Still others have used heaven as a pious escape from the responsibility of facing up to life; or they have made heaven into an Elysian island peopled by disembodied spirits and stacked with airy celestial furniture.

But to distort a concept is not to disprove its veracity; and if there were no hope of heaven our problems would be infinitely worse. The only accurate information we have about heaven is found in the Word of God. If we accept the authority of Scripture we may not know all we want to know about heaven, but we can be certain of some facts about it—facts which are clearly taught in the Biblical record:

Heaven is reality. Instead of being a fantasy-land of flitting shadows, heaven is where we will see and know the solid truth as it is. Heaven is built on facts. The perplexities and uncertainties and mysteries that trouble us to our dying hour will be cleared up in the presence of God. The mathematics of heaven is sound.

Heaven is beauty. The lovely things we know on this earth are only a foretaste of heaven. There will be music and color and unimaginable delights for those who enter the mansions God has prepared.

Heaven is joy. It is filled with marvelous people and they have marvelous times. Boredom and depression are unknown, as are the irritations, ailments, frustrations, disappointments and tragedies of this life. They all belong to the past.

Heaven is freedom. The restrictions and limitations of the flesh that impede life here will be lifted in heaven. We will no longer get in our own way. We will be released from our sins forever and be set free to live the abundant life.

Heaven is worship. Praising God is the vocation of heaven, and it takes many forms. Worshiping God means serving God, and heaven is a place of unlimited opportunity for activity that is useful to our heavenly Father.

Heaven is Communication. We shall speak the language of heaven, and know and be known, and understand and be understood. In fleeting moments Christians have known on earth what it is to have rich fellowship with each other and with the Lord Jesus Christ. That will be the order of the day in heaven.

Heaven is where Jesus is. The best has been saved till the last. This wonderful Person who has captivated men since He first walked the Mediterranean shore; who built a church that would withstand hell, and who conquered sin and death; He will be with us in heaven. We shall see Him as He is, face to face, and we shall be like Him.

What could be greater than that? Heaven is only part of the Christian life, but it is the last part and, from what we hear, the best.

Author Unknown

GOLdEN VERSE

O magic sleep! O comfortable bird
That broodest o'er the troubled sea of the
  mind
Till it is hushed and smooth.

John Keats

171

The Hand Of God

Our Father's hand is manifest
On mountain peak and plain,
From leaf to star, on rock-bound coast,
In rush of springtime rain;

Within the dell where violets
Bow heads as though in prayer,
And in the woods where rushing streams
Splash frocks the lilies wear.

We see God's signature upon
The desert's burning sand,
Where Silence speaks of wonders wrought
By His almighty hand!

Esther B. Heins

In His Good Time

I go to prove my soul,
I see my way as birds their trackless way,
I shall arrive. — What time, what circuit first,
I ask not: but unless God send His hail
Of blinding fireballs, sleet, or stifling snow,
In some time, His Good time, I shall arrive;
He guides me and the bird. In His good time.

Robert Browning

To One In Sorrow

Let me come in where you are weeping, friend,
And let me take your hand.
I, who have known a sorrow such as yours,
Can understand.
Let me come in—I would be very still
Beside you in your grief;
I would not bid you cease your weeping, friend,
Tears bring relief.
Let me come in—I would only breathe a prayer,
And hold your hand,
For I have known a sorrow such as yours,
And understand.

Grace Noll Crowell

GOLDEN VERSE

For age is opportunity no less
Than youth itself, though in another dress,
And as the evening twilight fades away
The sky is filled with stars, invisible by day.

Henry Wadsworth Longfellow

Life Is Forever! Death Is A Dream!

If we did not go to sleep at night
We'd never awaken to see the light.
And the joy of watching a new day break
Or meeting the dawn by some quiet lake
Would never be ours unless we slept
While God and all His angels kept
A vigil through this "little death"
That's over with the morning's breath —
And death, too, is a time of sleeping,
For those who die are in God's keeping
And there's a "suprise" for each soul.
For LIFE and DEATH is God's promised goal —
So trust God's promise and doubt Him never
For only through death can man LIVE FOREVER!

Helen Steiner Rice

The Gentle Gardener

I'd like to leave but daffodills to mark my little way,
To leave but tulips red and white behind me as I stray;
I'd like to pass away from earth and feel I'd left behind
But roses and forget-me-nots for all who come to find.

I'd like to sow the barren spots with all the flowers of earth,
To leave a path where those who come should find but gentle mirth;
And when at last I'm called upon to join the heavenly throng
I'd like to feel along my way I'd left no sign of wrong.

And yet the cares are many and the hours of toil are few;
There is not time enough on earth for all I'd like to do;
But, having lived and having toiled, I'd like the world to find
Some little touch of beauty that my soul had left behind.

Edgar A. Guest

As We Grow Older

A little more tired at close of day;
A little less anxious to have our way;
A little less ready to scold and blame;
A little more care of a brother's name;

And so we are nearing the journey's end,
Where time and eternity meet and blend.
And so we are faring adown the way
That leads to the gates of a better day.

A little more laughter, a few more tears,
And we shall have told our increasing years.
The book is closed and the prayers are said,
And we are part of the countless dead.

And so we are going, where all must go,
To the place the living may never know.
Thrice happy if then some soul can say,
"I'm better because he passed my way."

Rollin J. Wells

Twilight

The soft gray twilight slowly falls,
And sunset fades far in the west;
The world is wrapped in solemn hush,
Proclaiming now the hour of rest.

Softly a vesper bell is heard,
Stealing across the woodland deep . . .
Its rich tones soothe the tired heart,
Lulling the dying day to sleep.

Let it be so when my hour comes,
The hour of my unknown day . . .
May there be peace as sweet as this,
With one lone lark to guide my way.

William Arnette Wofford

ACKNOWLEDGMENTS *continued from page IV*

DOUBLEDAY & COMPANY, INC. for "A Christmas Miracle" from *Dare To Be Happy* by Helen Lowrie Marshall. Copyright © 1962 by Helen Lowrie Marshall. Also, for "Open Your Eyes" by E. B. Whisenand from A. L. Alexander's *Treasurehouse of Inspirational Poetry and Prose.* Copyright © 1966 by A. L. Alexander. Also, for "Leave A Touch of Glory", "A Bit of Eternity", "Thanksgiving Day", "New Friends", "Footprints In the Snow", "A Shaft of Sunlight" all from *Leave A Touch Of Glory* by Helen Lowrie Marshall. Copyright © 1976 by John Stanley Marshall as Executor of the Estate of Helen Lowrie Marshall. Reprinted by permission of Doubleday & Company, Inc.

FOUNDATION FOR CHRISTIAN LIVING for "Why the Christmas Bells Rang" by Norman Vincent Peale, adapted from a story by Raymond MacDonald Alden and published in the November 1976 issue of *Creative Help for Daily Living.* Copyright © 1976 by Foundation for Christian Living, Pawling, NY.

HARPER & ROW, PUBLISHERS, INC. for "To One In Sorrow" from *Songs of Hope* by Grace Noll Crowell. Copyright © 1938 by Harper & Row, Publishers, Inc.; renewed 1966 by Grace Noll Crowell. Reprinted by permission of the publisher.

HOPE B. FRIEDMANN for "I've Never Sailed the Seven Seas" and "Night Symphony" by Sue C. Boynton. Copyright © 1976 by Hope B. Friedmann. Used by permission.

GUIDEPOSTS for "The Sounion is Sinking" by Philip Griffin. Reprinted by permission from *Guideposts Magazine,* Copyright © 1974 by Guideposts Associates, Inc., Carmel, New York 10502.

HIGHLIGHTS FOR CHILDREN, INC. for "Mrs. McMinney and Her Children" by Marilyn Kratz, Copyright © 1974, *Highlights For Children, Inc.,* Columbus, Ohio. Also, for "Sandy's Unhappy Birthday" by Susan Goldman, Copyright © 1974, Highlights For Children, Inc., Columbus, Ohio.

THE JUDSON PRESS for "The Watchman Saw It Happen" from *Bible Stories to Tell* by Elizabeth Whitehouse, The Judson Press. Also, for "Zacchaeus Finds A Friend" from *Bible Stories to Tell* by Elizabeth Whitehouse, The Judson Press. Used by permission.

J. B. LIPPINCOTT COMPANY for "Standing by the Crib", from *Mince Pie* by Christopher Morley. Copyright © 1919, renewed 1947 by Christopher Morley. Reprinted by permission of J. B. Lippincott Company.

THE QUIET HOUR ECHOES for "Dad and Me Together" by Ottis Shirk, June 1976 issue, "Little Things", by Adam N. Reiter, June 1974 issue, "Mother" by N. O. Moore, May 1976 issue, "Thanks Be to God" by Marylene Hubert, November 1976 issue, and "What Jesus Did for Me", November 1975 issue.

HENRY REGNERY COMPANY for "The Gentle Gardener" by Edgar A. Guest.

FLEMING H. REVELL COMPANY for "A Parable of Life" by Perry Tanksley from *Love Gift . . . Because I Like You.* Fleming H. Revell Company.

THE SATURDAY EVENING POST for "Bright Fragment" by Theodosia Benjamin.

SCM PRESS LTD. for "In God's Hands" by A. Herbert Gray from *The Secret of Inward Peace* by A. Herbert Gray, SCM Press 1947.

TIME INCORPORATED for "George Washington" and "Abraham Lincoln", from *TIME Special Report, The American Presidents.*

THE UPPER ROOM for "Just A Moment Longer" by Violet Munro from *Images: Women in Transition.* Copyright © 1976 by The Upper Room. Reprinted by permission of The Upper Room.

ZONDERVAN PUBLISHING HOUSE for "The Precious Friend" from *Sourcebook of Poetry* compiled by Al Bryant.

WE ALSO WISH TO THANK

the following contributors and sources for their permission to reprint selections in this book:

Betty F. Anderson, Ann L. Bangham, Bernadine Beatie, Viola J. Berg, Rev. George E. Blanchard, Sr., Loretta Bowser, Sue C. Boynton, Ester York Burkholder, Martin Buxbaum, Dorothy Cahoon, Georgia R. Cameron, Leota Campbell, Lucille Crumley, Marianna Rossi Decker, Eleanor DiGiulio, Nelia M. Dosser, Grace E. Easley, Gwen Frostic, Paul Hamsher, Joseph A. Harris, Ester B. Heins, Phyllis M. Hemphill, Jerome Hines, IDEAS UN-LIMITED, Ruby Jones, Louise Justice, Rhena S. LaFever, Roger Kerr, Ruby Maschke, Violet Munro, Katherine T. Paxson, Pearl Polosky, Beulah H. Ragland, REILLY, LEE AND CO., Helen Steiner Rice, Dale Evans Rogers, Garnett Ann Schultz, Ralph W. Seager, SIGNS OF THE TIMES, Jean Conder Soule, Louise Weibert Sutton, SUNSHINE MAGA-ZINE, Alice Mackenzie Swaim, Joseph D. Tonkin, Gloria L. Vaughan, Annette Victorin, William Arthur Ward, Harriet C. Whipple, Viney Wilder, Mrs. William A. Wofford, Miriam Woolfolk.

WE ALSO WISH TO THANK

those contributors from whom we were unable to obtain a response prior to publication:
Velta Myrle Allen, The Australian Evangel, Gerald C. Barton, Rowena Bennett, Johnielu Barber Bradford, Barbara Burrow, Esther Lee Carter, Marie Daerr, Eunice Fields, Herbert Gray; Harcourt, Brace Jovanovich, Inc.; Roger Kerr, John Knox Press, Kritina Metcalfe Lewis, Macmillan Company, Paul S. McElroy, Thomas Nelson, Inc., Reader's Digest Association, H. M. S. Richards, Heywood Skinner, Virginia Vess, Tessa S. Webb, Young Americans Riding Into History, Inc.

Diligent effort has been made to locate and secure permission for the inclusion of all copyrighted material in this book. If any such acknowledgments have been inadvertently omitted, the compilers and publishers would appreciate receiving full information so that proper credit may be given in future editions.

Arthur S. DeMoss

Traun Lake, Austria